JOHN UPDIKE

By ROBERT DETWEILER

Emory University

BOBBS-MERRILL EDUCATIONAL PUBLISHING

INDIANAPOLIS

Library of Congress Catalog Card Number 74-187611

ISBN 0-672-61506-1

Cover Art by Richard Listenberger

MANUFACTURED IN THE UNITED STATES OF AMERICA

96 8 29

In memory of my father: my Chiron

Contents

Preface

A CRITICAL study of a contemporary author presents unique problems. One is tempted to judge him in terms of the immediate impression he makes, even while seeking the crystallizations of history and accumulated opinion. In using bibliographical resources, one must depend less upon contemplative, measured books and essays and more on ephemeral reviews and literary gossip. There is, moreover, far less opportunity to notice change, progression, the development of general patterns in a current author's career than in that of one whose life and work are established in a past era.

The situation is doubly difficult when the study has to do with a prolific novelist such as John Updike who doesn't stand still long enough to be properly observed. His poems, stories, and reviews appear regularly in various magazines; he is interviewed frequently and offers his comments about many matters; he is the subject (and victim) of intensifying critical attention. Above all, even though he has been publishing fiction for some fifteen years, he is just now in early middle age and has perhaps not yet written his most significant work.

All of this is good, in a way. It forces one to expend less effort on the social-cultural implications of his writing and more on a comprehension and appreciation of his fiction as art. Much of the negative criticism directed at Updike simply ignores his technical ability and labels his fiction as unimportant because it does not deal dramatically with life's great issues. Yet he is a fine craftsman whose skill with the language of narrative must be considered before one can speak intelligently about his social and cultural relevance. Updike does treat the great issues, and he does so in a manner that deserves attention; but his is not a strategy that is recognizable in any other author or literary movement. If Updike can be classified at all in terms of literary traditions, one might say that he writes a "secular baroque." It is elaborate, texture-conscious, structurally balanced, highly controlled, mythically resonant fiction, yet a kind that does not celebrate such a rich and ordered world but instead ironically marks its passing.

My intention in this study is to demonstrate the qualities of irony and self-consciousness inherent in the art of "secular baroque." I have attempted explications in depth of his six novels published to date by showing how their mythic (and post-mythic) patterns relate to a disjunctive modern reality, causing an ironic awareness to emerge. In discussing Updike's four short-story collections (I include *Bech: A Book* among these), I have paid more attention to individual configurations of behavior and to the introspective reactions they incite. Since the four collections present a fairly clear sequence of human maturation—from child protagonists to adults in their thirties and forties—the mythic depth (present in the short stories but less pronounced than in the novels) is partially replaced here by the range of self-analytical characters.

This study is, therefore, exclusively one of Updike's fiction; but I have drawn upon his discursive prose here and there to elucidate a novel or story. I have not attempted to analyze his essays and reviews. They are lucid and self-evident and need no interpretation. Apart from introducing each chapter with a line or more of his poetry, I have not explicated his verse. His first two poetry collections consist mainly of light-hearted word and rhythm games that he himself, I think, would not wish to have taken seriously. His third collection, *Midpoint and Other Poems,* does contain serious and competent verse; but I have had to draw the line somewhere in choosing from the wealth of material to discuss; and I decided to draw it at the natural boundary between fiction and poetry.

At places where it seemed especially appropriate I have commented on the relationships between Updike's life and his fiction; but I have, for the most part, avoided biographical interpretation. We are, presumably, more interested in what he has written than in the circumstances behind the writing.

I have commented on all of Updike's collected stories, but I have not analyzed any of the uncollected pieces.

A word, finally, on my use of secondary sources. Updike criticism has been growing rapidly in the past decade, and some of it is very good indeed (as my annotated bibliography indicates); yet I have used little of it in the preparation and actual writing of my study. No "schools" of Updike criticism worth reporting on have arisen at this stage. One can at best identify a group of reviewers given to a consistent belittling of

Preface

Updike (John Aldridge, Leslie Fiedler, William Gass, Norman Podhoretz) and another group that offers qualified praise (Richard Gilman, Granville Hicks, Arthur Mizener). Although I refer to the negative critics on occasion, I have not tried to answer their arguments individually, for those arguments rest on broad assertions (i.e., that Updike will not accept the challenge of "big" themes) that my study as a whole denies.

In addition, only one book-length study has appeared to date among the proliferation of reviews and essays on Updike. An attempt to summarize and characterize this array of criticism, therefore, could do little to counteract the sense of fragmentation and would certainly result in a different kind of study than this series represents.

I am indebted to Professor Sylvia E. Bowman for her skillful editing of the manuscript and to Elizabeth Stopinski for help of many kinds while the study was in progress.

ROBERT DETWEILER

Emory University

Acknowledgments

Permission has been granted to reprint the poem "Mirror" from THE CARPENTERED HEN AND OTHER TAME CREATURES by John Updike. Copyright © 1957 by John Updike. Originally appeared in *The New Yorker* as "Reflections," and reprinted by permission of Harper & Row, Publishers.

Permission has also been granted by Harper & Row, Publishers to quote from the poems "Tao in the Yankee Stadium Bleachers" and "Room 28," which appear in THE CARPENTERED HEN AND OTHER TAME CREATURES by John Updike. Copyright © 1956, 1957 by John Updike.

Permission has been granted by Alfred A. Knopf, Inc., to quote from "Suburban Madrigal," "Earthworm," "Thoughts While Driving Home," "Shillington," "Movie House," "Seven Stanzas at Easter," and "Erotic Epigrams." These poems appear in TELEPHONE POLES AND OTHER POEMS by John Updike. Copyright © 1958, 1959, 1960, 1961, 1962, 1963 by John Updike.

Permission has been granted by Alfred A. Knopf, Inc., to quote from the poem "Fireworks," which appears in MIDPOINT AND OTHER POEMS by John Updike. Copyright © 1964 by John Updike.

Permission has been granted by Alfred A. Knopf, Inc., to quote from the book reviews "Creatures of the Air," and "More Love in the Western World" which appear in ASSORTED PROSE by John Updike. Copyright © 1961, 1963, by John Updike.

Permission has been granted by John Updike to quote from "The Dogwood Tree: A Boyhood," which appears in ASSORTED PROSE by John Updike. Copyright © 1962 by Martin Levin.

Chronology

1932   John Updike born in Shillington, Pennsylvania.

1936-   Attended Shillington public schools.
1950

1945   Moved with family to a farm in Plowville, Pennsylvania.

1950   Entered Harvard University.

1953   Married Mary Pennington.

1954   Was graduated *summa cum laude* (with a major in English) from Harvard; sold first story ("Friends from Philadelphia") to *The New Yorker.*

1954-   Attended the Ruskin School of Drawing and Fine Arts in
1955   Oxford, England, on a Knox Fellowship.

1955   Daughter Elizabeth born.

1955-   Worked as a staff writer for *The New Yorker* and wrote some
1957   of "The Talk of the Town" columns.

1957   Son David born; moved with family to Ipswich, Massachusetts.

1958   Collected poems, *The Carpentered Hen,* published; *The Poorhouse Fair* published.

1959   Son Michael born; *The Same Door* published.

1960   Daughter Miranda born; received Rosenthal Award of the National Institute of Arts and Letters for *The Poorhouse Fair; Rabbit, Run* published.

1962   *Pigeon Feathers and Other Stories* published.

1963   *Telephone Poles and Other Poems* published; *The Centaur* published.

1964   Received National Book Award for *The Centaur;* elected member of the National Institute of Arts and Letters; *Olinger Stories, A Selection* published.

1964-   Traveled to Russia, Rumania, Bulgaria, and Czechoslovakia
1965   as part of the U.S.S.R.-U.S. Cultural Exchange Program.

1965   *Of the Farm* and *Assorted Prose* published.

1966   *The Music School* published; received First O. Henry Prize for "The Bulgarian Poetess."

1968   *Couples* published.

1969   *Midpoint and Other Poems* published.

1970   *Bech: A Book* published.

1971   *Rabbit Redux* published.

CHAPTER 1

The Same Door:
Unexpected Gifts

We have one home, the first, and leave that one.
The having and leaving go on together.
—from "Shillington"[1]

I *Grace and Epiphanies*

THE SAME DOOR, published in 1959, is a collection of sixteen short stories written over a period of five years and originally published, some in different form, in *The New Yorker*; and they represent various stages of Updike's maturity. The first story, "Friends from Philadelphia," was also Updike's first commercially published fiction, written in 1954 after his graduation from Harvard. The others were composed during his 1955 scholarship year at Oxford, during his two-year tenure as *New Yorker* staff writer (1955-57), and during his first two years as an independent novelist. Consequently, the stories have little formal unity as a collection, and any attempt to generalize about them is confounded by exceptions.

Certain aspects of casual unity are created by a consistent authorial attitude toward life and by a recurrent structural technique. Updike himself articulates the attitude in the foreword to a later collection called *Olinger Stories*. Answering the complaint that one of those stories seems to have no point, he comments "The point, to me, is plain, and is the point, more or less, of all these Olinger stories. *We are rewarded unexpectedly*. The muddled and inconsequent surface of things now and then parts to yield us a gift."[2] This point is the one made as well, if sometimes negatively so, in the *The Same Door*; and it expresses a conviction of the author that becomes more determinative as the body of his fiction grows. Updike is a Chris-

15

tian, if not a "religious" writer in the accepted sense, and the centrality of grace in the Protestant experience finds its way into his art through the expression of the gift or the reward.

The particular unifying technique is similar to the construction of the Joycean "epiphany," at least according to the way in which that much-debated term has been generally understood. Somewhat as in Joyce's *Dubliners, The Same Door* stories, instead of attempting the brutal surprise or the psychological shock, concentrate on producing the gradual revelation—the culminating knowledge-plus-emotion that dawns upon the protagonist following his crucial experiences and upon the reader after he has finished the story. Also, as in Joyce's stories, Updike's epiphanies, while they do not depend upon an overt religious context (except in "Dentistry and Doubt"), translate fundamentally religious or at least moral experiences into artistic imagery and action. The revelatory moment does not result from any sensational conflicts or climactic scenes, for these are not stories of deep passion, violence, or death. They occur in the midst of daily life, mixing with the stuff of the mundane; and the insight slowly materializes through a fine fusion of memories, reflexes, and some subtle catalyst of the unexpected. Against the wonted beat of familial or vocational being, a counterpoint insinuates itself in these stories that at last upsets the rhythm and forces the characters and reader to pause and then to reconsider the whole composition.

II   *"Friends from Philadelphia"*

Although the sixteen stories span a period from the very beginning of Updike's career to his establishment as a respected young artist, one finds little difference in the quality of the fiction. "Friends from Philadelphia," the first tale, shows some evidence of a neophyte author in search of a style; but the result is not a weak story by any means: it is, at its worst, a narrative that does not sound like the later, familiar Updike. The sentences are often short and choppy, dialogue predominates, and very little of the metaphoric interplay that marks the later fiction is present. The story succeeds, however, along other lines. Through careful characterization via dialogue, Updike reveals the sensitive uncertainty of late adolescence in contrast to the bluff confidence of adults who have located their secure little niches in society.

The tale is simple enough. Fifteen-year-old John Nordholm, who lives a mile outside Olinger, hikes into town to buy the wine that his parents need to entertain expected guests from Philadelphia. Since he is too young to buy alcohol, he stops by the Lutz home and asks if the father will buy it for him. Mr. Lutz himself arrives home later slightly drunk and agrees to drive John and the teenage Lutz daughter to the liquor store. He allows John (underage) to drive the new family car to the store, takes John's two dollars, and soon reappears with the wine. When they arrive at the Nordholm house, John asks hesitantly for his change and receives it along with the bottle. As Lutz and his daughter drive away, young John Nordholm discovers that the wine is Château Mouton-Rothschild 1937.

The charm of the story, along with the semi-sophisticated banter between the teenagers and the description of the television-addicted Mrs. Lutz in her darkened room, is in the ambivalent kindness of Mr. Lutz. His is an unexpectedly gracious act, for the wine obviously cost much more than the innocent boy anticipated; and the man does not humiliate him in front of the snide daughter by refusing to give change or by divulging the quality and price of the wine. But his gesture is also a patronizing one that increases Mr. Lutz's self-esteem at the expense of the Nordholms. John's schoolteacher-father can't afford good wine or a new car as the uneducated but prosperous Mr. Lutz can, and young John is left with the ironic reward. He is gifted for his family's poverty but suffers condescension for it as well. The revelation of the story, therefore, is that kindness has its price, perhaps, and that receiving grace demands its own kind of maturity.

III "Ace in the Hole"

The second narrative, "Ace in the Hole," could be a preliminary sketch for *Rabbit, Run.* Fred "Ace" Anderson, like Harry Angstrom, is a twenty-six-year-old ex-high school basketball star, married, father of a small child, and the sad product of maternal domination. On the particular day of the story, he has been fired from his job—not for the first time—as a used-car salesman; and he returns home to await the arrival of his working wife and to appease somehow her anticipated anger at his latest failure. The story is packed with the complications and

baggage of young American marriage. Evey, the wife, is Roman
Catholic; and Ace is Protestant—a sore point between them.
Their life is saturated with TV, pop music, beer, and the
omnipresent cigarettes. They appear to have married directly
out of high school when they were too young and when they
had developed no skills; and they survive in a precarious finan-
cial state. Evey has matured, but Ace has not. He lives in the
illusion of his teenage glory and is a childish egotist. Updike
describes in detail how Ace lovingly combs his long, sleek hair
in front of the mirror; and he stresses that, while Ace has just
lost his job—a reason for actual concern—he is really bothered
because a mention of his high-scoring record in the local sports
news that day has employed his name of Fred instead of Ace.

That evening Evey takes rather stoically the news of the firing
(Ace's mother has already told her), but the irresponsible young
husband soon irritates her into bitter recriminations. Then Ace
turns on his charm. He distracts her by applauding their baby
daughter's antics, then persuades her to dance with him to the
sound of dinner music on the radio. The tale ends with the two
of them, everything unresolved, dancing a quickening swing
step in the isolation of the drab apartment, trying pathetically
to relive the popularity of their carefree high school days.

Updike has, amazingly, already found his métier in "Ace in
the Hole." The story offers less in terms of plot and action than
"Friends from Philadelphia" but much more in terms of pure
mood created out of sheer verbal craftsmanship. It is, much
like *Rabbit, Run*, a sustained metaphor of nervous movement
and a tension of opposites. Ace is always in motion: driving
the car, smoking hastily, tapping a foot in rhythm, running
home from his mother's house with the small daughter in his
arms—still shifting restlessly on life's basketball court, trying
to score and to be the hero again with the effortlessness of the
natural. But Ace is not a natural in the workaday world. An
indulgent mother and cheap early fame have spoiled him, and
he is already a clearcut failure at the approaching prime of
life. The antagonistic characters, his opposites, make his plight
the more obvious. The prowling high school youths who insult
him at the traffic light only show him (like the boys playing
back-alley basketball at the start of *Rabbit, Run*) the reckless
innocence that he has lost. His weary and dispirited wife, with
her dogged common sense, makes him seem more of a loser.

Apart from a sexual innuendo, the title has a double sense. The protagonist is Ace "in the hole": jobless, unprepared to be a man, and threatened with a spouse nearly ready to leave him. But he also *has* his ace in the hole: his animal charm and his instincts that will help him to survive even if he ruins others in the process. The story is an inversion of the maturation pattern, for the events that should jolt the initiate into growing up at last only cause him to fight reality with a wasteful nervous energy. "Ace in the Hole" seems authentic because it fashions a modern American type, the teenage hero seduced by quick success into thinking that the adult world is easy to conquer but who soon suffers disillusion and the gradual degeneration into bumhood. Olinger can be too kind, the family-community can be too generous, when it offers its sons what they should strive a lifetime to deserve—and then permits grace to turn quickly into judgment. Updike has forced more news about one dead end along the American way of life into one brief story than many writers manage to report in a whole novel. It is no wonder that he returned to the theme and the place and expanded the microform into *Rabbit, Run.*

IV   *"Tomorrow and Tomorrow and So Forth"*

In this tale (the third in the collection), young Mark Prosser is teaching *Macbeth* to a class of restless eleventh-graders; the narration is third-person, from Prosser's point of view. Updike's later familiar blending of the lofty and the trivial (on which *The Centaur* is based) appears here for the first time with clarity. It is carried in the title: "Tomorrow and Tomorrow and So Forth" joins the beginning of the famous Shakespearean soliloquy with the callous teenage disregard for highflown language, just as the inane teenage paraphrases of the speech clash with the quite incisive analysis that Prosser gives the bored students—and that is lost, of course, on them. That incongruity, introduced by the pupils' barbarizing of a classic, is deepened and then justified and resolved in the central action of the story.

Just before the period is over, Prosser intercepts a note passed from the provocative Gloria Angstrom to a boyfriend in which she confesses that "He's heavenly with poetry. I think I love him. I really do *love* him." Prosser detains the girl after class and lectures to her firmly but kindly about the dangers of using love's vocabulary too lightly; she leaves on the verge of tears. Immediately after, while Prosser is enjoying this surprising evidence of his professional-masculine charm, another teacher enters to tell him the gossip of the day: Gloria has written the same sort of note about two other faculty members and had them purposely discovered. Prosser has obviously been duped, and he is angered by the girl's duplicity; but he also comprehends that the trick has backfired on her: "The girl had been almost crying; he was sure of that."

Updike manages to project, in the unpredictable extremes of a youthful mind, a pettiness and a potential nobility that contribute together to the imaged truths of the story. As Prosser discovers, "a terrible tenderness" marks adolescents; and that oxymoron contains the power of the narrative. A young girl can use her budding sexuality to play an irritating trick on her instructors, but she will also respond to an honest encounter. The experience holds a gift for pupil and teacher. He takes her seriously, in their private discussion after class, in spite of her immaturity; and she answers with an acknowledgment of respect for him that was hidden hitherto behind the façade of mischief. "This petty pace from day to day" is quickened and made worthwhile by the occasional spontaneous meeting of two momentarily unmasked selves.

V "Snowing in Greenwich Village"

"Snowing in Greenwich Village," the seventh of *The Same Door* series, is one of the most impressive performances in the collection. It shifts from the Olinger setting to Manhattan and introduces Richard and Joan Maple, a young married couple who appear again, older and unhappier, in *The Music School* and in four uncollected short stories.[3] Very little actually happens in the narration; instead, it shows the author absorbed in his persistent but delicate probing of interacting personalities. Richard (in the advertising trade) and Joan have just moved to West Thirteenth Street in the Village and have invited an old acquaintance over for the evening, Rebecca Cune, a girl with "a gift for odd things."

The three drink sherry and converse, but the talk is dominated by Rebecca's wry recollections of the strange people she has known. Joan, who has a cold and has not been at all witty in the conversation, is roused by the clatter of horses of mounted policemen. She rushes to the window, sees snow falling outside, and hugs her husband in a moment of unguarded intimacy while their guest watches blandly. When Rebecca leaves, Richard walks her home and follows her upstairs, aroused, to see her apartment. At her door as he prepares to leave, they are poised to embrace; but Richard destroys the critical moment with a joke that misfires, and departs.

The undertone of sexual competition pervades the tale. Joan and Rebecca are at cautious odds from the start, and Updike contrasts them graphically: Joan's angular "Modiglianiesque" features give her an air of simplicity, but Rebecca is a da Vinci type whose constant enigmatic smile reminds one of the mystery of the tantalizing Mona Lisa portrait. Beneath the purposefully casual conversation, one is made to feel the unnamed struggle. Richard is the prize, Joan the defender of her property, and Rebecca the predator. Joan's weapon is her defenselessness; Rebecca's, her cool and cryptic reserve that promises a hidden excitement. Richard is caught between loyalty toward his wife, who is put at a disadvantage by the off-beat discussion, and Rebecca's novel attractiveness. The chatting remains discreet, but the adultery motif accompanies it through the repeated references to beds: in the first paragraph, Richard lays Rebecca's coat and scarf on their marriage bed; Rebecca relaxes on the floor in the living room with her arm on the Hide-a-Bed (while Joan sits straightbacked on a chair); Rebecca tells about the bedroom troubles she had in sharing her apartment with a pair of lovers; and, when Richard at the end visits her apartment, he is surprised to see the double bed that dominates the room. The subtlety of the imagery matches the subtlety of the invitation to extra-marital adventure.

But Rebecca's strength is also her weakness. Her knack for comic recitation gradually emerges as the extent of her substance. She achieves her unique personality at the expense of others, exaggerating their foibles to fit the style of her performance. That Rebecca is a predator in every way Richard suddenly grasps after his wife's impulsive embrace, as he sees Joan and himself from Rebecca's viewpoint. She will twist the moment of tenderness into a joke when she narrates the scene to other friends: the simple wife with the sniffles who hugs her husband in ludicrous joy because it happens to be snowing. But Richard's discovery does not make her less desirable; for when Richard escorts her home (at Joan's insistence—a smart if risky strategy, since it forces her opponent's move), they hold an embarrassed dialogue that masks the tension of pre-sexual encounter and that continues inside her apartment.

Updike produces the tension by allowing the inane comments to fill the void of anticipation. The crucial moment, exquisitely described, occurs at the door when Richard acts to leave; and the result could go either way. Rebecca, very close to him in the shadows, is waiting for him to make the move. If he does, he betrays his wife; if he doesn't, he becomes the ridiculous male. He tries a joke and stutters; the timing and the situation are ruined. He is free but at the expense of his pride.

Since this is Richard Maple's story, one must inquire what unexpected gift he receives. It may be, in part, the thrill of the just-missed extra-marital adventure; but, more likely, it is that he does *not* become intimately involved. He has had the quick glance into the tantalizing maze of illicit romance but also the luck, or the grace, to avoid its penalties—emotional, social, and moral. The revelation of mutual attraction between a man and a woman is a joy not only because it reassures one of his desirability but also because it indicates an elementary kind of human communication. A fine line may exist between lust and love, but the libido need not always incite to sexual consummation; it can produce other kinds of knowledge as well. Lust can teach.

VI   "A Gift from the City"

The thirteenth story, "A Gift from the City," employs the technique of inversion. James and Liz are a well-to-do young couple with a baby daughter who live on Tenth Street in Greenwich Village. Liz telephones her husband at work on a Friday afternoon to tell him that a poor Negro from North Carolina has been at her door asking for work and that she has given him ten dollars and sent him away. But the man wants to come back on Saturday evening to thank the husband as well for their generosity. That prospect upsets James; and, when the Negro

actually does appear the next evening, James in his embarrassment gives him twenty dollars more. James and Liz are afraid
now that they have a permanent dole on their hands and are
not sure if they should believe his story: that he has just arrived
from the South with wife and family and has a construction
job promised him for the following week. Friends of the couple
argue that the man is a fraud. When James returns home
from work on Monday evening, Liz informs him that the Negro
has been there once more, and that she sent him away without
any money. He does not appear again, and the equilibrium of
their life is restored.

The title is double-edged and signifies the inversion that
gives the story its rationale. James tells the Negro to accept
the thirty dollars from them "as a gift from the city." What he
and his wife do not see, in their genteel materialist pride, is that
the Negro himself is the real gift from the city to them. Whether
he is a small-time swindler or someone in genuine need, he is
involved in a struggle for survival; and he is offered to them as
a unique introduction to the destitution that characterizes the
other side of metropolitan living. But James and Liz, for all
their humanitarian impulses and notions of decency, do not
really want to *know* the Negro. James is insulted when the black
man refers to them as his only friends in New York. The scene
in which James sees a similarity between the Negro's head and
a new shaver he has designed is revealing. James is immersed in
a world of things, and philanthropy must remain nicely objective and distant in that schema. He is easy prey for panhandlers
on the street because he is so acutely fearful of a personal
involvement that will unbalance his neatly arranged way of life.

James thinks twice of magic circles around his wife and
child that would protect them from the hundred daily dangers
of Manhattan living. In the first reference, he is sorry that love
is too immaterial to protect his dearest ones; but, by the end of
the story, in his frustration over the resilient Negro, he believes
that he has "sold his life, his chances" for his wife's sake and
that she should make her own enchanted circles. But love in
this story is too dependent on the modern symbols of affluence
for its effectiveness and is perhaps more a matter of egotistic
possession than of shared affection. In any case, James and Liz
are in a charmed circle that they have unwittingly drawn around
themselves and from which they cannot escape. Because of

their economic and social success, they are separated from much
of the real humanity of the city. In spite of their broadminded-
ness, they are morally narrow; they have chosen not to help;
and, through their wealth, they are made spiritually poor. To
be able to give graciously is also a gift; and the couple, by
refusing to meet the Negro in all his potential, are denying
themselves the gift they most need.

VII   *"The Happiest I've Been"*

If "A Gift from the City" concludes with an ironic word
about peace of mind and moral compromise, "The Happiest
I've Been," the final story of the collection, returns with con-
siderable nostalgia to the context of a fading moral innocence.
John Nordholm (as Updike states it in the Foreword to *Olinger
Stories*), having taken his turn as protagonist in "Friends from
Philadelphia," narrates the story in the first person as a nineteen-
year-old college student who is home in Olinger for the Christmas vacation. The tale is stylistically different from the others
in *The Same Door*. It is essentially plotless and has the form
of a reminiscence, a series of smoothly connected vignettes
that one would guess to be transposed autobiography—Updike's personally experienced Shillington into the fictive Olinger of 1951. Yet the story evokes a mood that marks a transitional stage in one's maturing rather than a specific history
and geography. It is the period of the end of youthful innocence, when one practices the rites of adulthood half-willingly
to demonstrate sophistication, yet lingers with the more familiar
and less complicated habits of late adolescence.

John is picked up in the evening by Neil, a friend of his,
to drive to a girlfriend's New Year's party in Chicago, seven-
teen hours distant; but, once beyond parental ken, they decide
to attend first in Olinger a party given by former high school
classmates. They stay at the party until three in the morning
and then take two girls home to nearby Riverside. Margaret,
one of the girls, invites the others into her parents' home for
early coffee; while Neil and the other girl pet in the darkened
house, John and Margaret sit and talk until she falls asleep in
his arm. As dawn breaks, the two boys finally leave for Chicago.
Neil has John drive the car and sleeps beside him as the trip
begins.

Except for "A Gift from the City," this is the longest story of the collection and one of Updike's favorites—a fact that in itself does not necessarily insure its quality; but the author does achieve his artistic ends through control of narrative idiom, perspective, and manipulation of an efficient metaphoric pattern. John tells the story in a retrospective late-teenager style —one relatively free of Updike's now ripened elaborate diction —that infuses his experience with a simple, forthright authenticity. But the angle of vision is not therefore wholly a teenager's; it is a double view that tempers the precious hours of the youthful past with the increased wisdom of the present.

The result is a certain discrepancy of moods and tones that creates the sense of loss now beginning to invade Updike's fiction and appearing strongest in *The Centaur* and *The Music School*. This mood is indicated in the adverbial superlative of the title ("The *Happiest* I've Been") and in the shadow of sadness that lingers over the careful description. Updike quotes Henri Bergson in the preface to *The Same Door*: "How many of our present pleasures, were we to examine them closely, would shrink into nothing more than memories of past ones!" That realization, which applies exactly to this story, is also Wordsworthian: with increasing self-consciousness comes the loss of natural, spontaneous joy, so that the stylizing mind must reconstruct its pleasures artificially out of the past.

But even if that much of the romantic survives in Updike, he possesses the discipline to fashion a universally meaningful event out of a private memory and to create thereby sentiment instead of sentimentality. "The Happiest I've Been" broadens into a modern maturation ritual, replete with the archetypal accoutrements, that does not simply dress up the old forms of twentieth-century art but also adds a new interpretive dimension. The season, the party, and the trip embody and symbolize the transitional nature of the experience that introduces a new stage of maturity. It is nearly New Year (the classmates pretend that it *is* New Year's Eve), the time to begin formally a fresh kind of existence; and the trip has echoes of the *rite de passage*. John leaves the old farm and his gnarled grandmother and aging parents for young, robust Chicago and the girlfriend awaiting him there; and, of course, the actual journey begins at the pristine moment of dawn. It is an emphatic moment of separation from family and home and the start of the independent journey through adult life.

The party particularly has ritual elements. It is a last meeting in youthful irresponsibility; less a reunion than a final celebration of oneness; still held in a parental home, but in one from which the parents are absent. The games, the alcoholic drinks, the dancing, all combined with a constant awareness of *the time*, blend the playfulness of adolescence with the growing sophistication of impending adulthood. When at midnight "everyone" tries to kiss the only married girl of the group, the concentrated ritual duality becomes most apparent; it is an embracing of the new state of being attempted through a playful gesture.

The new relevance of the maturation pattern appears after the party among the privacy of the two couples. The movement is from the group to individuals, from the tribe to self-conscious formal structures. For John Nordholm, the revelation of beginning maturity that promises goodness for the future and that makes him the happiest he's been comes through the double incident of demonstrated faith that others have in him: "There was knowing that twice since midnight a person had trusted me enough to fall asleep beside me." The nostalgia for an irretrievable carefree past is balanced by a pride in the assumed responsibility of adult relationships. One trusts one's sexual being, one's safety, with the other person; and there is joy in accepting the burden of that faith.

Here once more, finally, is the theme of the unexpected gift that runs through all the stories. To be treated as an adult, and the ability to respond as one, are two of life's subtle presents; to be introduced to the challenges of manhood through the expressed new trust of old friends is a surprising graciousness of nature, or of fate. Indeed, Updike might interpret it as an extension of God's blessing into one's deepening self-conscious existence.

VIII   *Variations on the Themes*

The other stories in the collection present variations on the themes and motifs already described. "Dentistry and Doubt" concerns an American divinity student at Oxford who, plagued by Luther-like struggles with the devil, finds solace in a visit to an English dentist when the man working on his teeth prompts him into recalling a faith-restoring quotation. The story ends with an apt natural metaphor: as the student watches birds through the window, he sees two wrens snatch a crumb from a blackbird—like a pair of weak humans outsmarting Satan.

In "The Kid's Whistling," a young commercial artist who is working overtime during the Christmas season and who is annoyed by the incessant piping of a stockboy is paid a touchy visit in his department-store office by his impatient wife. She leaves, he ruins the TOYLAND sign he was lettering, and discovers it was because "the kid had stopped whistling." The irritations of life, whether they are the minor bothers caused by fellow workers or the more constant frictions of marriage, become as familiar and as much second nature as the established comforts. They are also a kind of communication, and one learns to depend upon them to maintain the rhythms of human endeavor.

"Toward Evening," which is more of a sketch than a short story, is the only one of its kind in the book. Rafe, a young New Yorker, takes a bus home from work to his wife and baby daughter on the Upper West Side. Some undefined rift separates him and his wife that evening, and he retreats into whimsical, cynical conjecture about the pointless construction of the huge Spry sign that shines across from the New Jersey side of the Hudson River. When the gift of human response is not forthcoming, it seems, one feels himself abandoned in the mechanized and vulgar meaninglessness of the age.

"Who Made Yellow Roses Yellow?" contrasts the suave Manhattan playboy Fred Platt with his old Ivy League classmate Clayton Clayton, the middle-class plodder who has made good as a big business executive. Just returned from France, Platt wants a job with Clayton's firm but is too proud to ask directly. When they meet for lunch, Fred offers hints that Clayton, still dazzled by his friend's worldly-wise front, doesn't take seriously. Frustrated by his failure, Fred insults the bewildered Clayton with school-primer French as they separate. Fred Platt is one of Updike's few thoroughly unpleasant character creations (Freddy Thorne in *Couples* is a more recent one), but he is also pathetic. Caught in the web of his own perverse personality, he cannot really meet anyone else on honest terms; and he seems doomed to isolation in his shallow social superiority. Even the last name (Platt is German for "flat" or "low") reinforces the sense of underlying failure.

"Sunday Teasing," in turn, is a subtly cruel story of a marriage relationship; and Updike uses in it the trick of fiction within fiction to impose the effect. The young couple Arthur and Macy, after a discussion about family affection with their Sunday dinner guest, retire for the evening; and Macy reads a depressing French short story that she passes on to her husband. He explains its essence to her—it concerns a "perceptive man caged in his own weak character"—and he then defends the hero's apparently harsh treatment of the heroine. When Macy begins to cry in confusion, Arthur humors her and puts her to bed. One realizes gradually that Arthur is also very aware but very weak, and the skillfully placed aspects of the story fall into line. Unamuno's *The Tragic Sense of Life* (which Arthur is reading), Arthur's distorted understanding of Protestant individuality, his playful demand that Macy mimic the Garbo line, "You're fooling me."—all these assume a terrible irony. Arthur does not, perhaps cannot, love his wife; but he doesn't have the courage to tell her. Instead, he keeps them both suspended in a painful illusion of communion. Behind his self-righteous Christian pose, he is sinning against her and himself.

In "His Finest Hour," George and Rosalind Chandler intervene in a bloody marital quarrel in a neighboring Manhattan apartment. A month later, they receive an extravagant gift of flowers from the neighbors "to show that everything was right between our families." The Chandlers move to Arabia; homesick for America, George's first vision is always of a profusion of flowers in the shabby West Side rooms. This is a story of the unexpected and unrecognized reward, but George Chandler's "finest hour" is not when he ends the quarrel but when he and his wife are the surprised recipients of the flowers from the people they had thought to despise.

In "A Trillion Feet of Gas," a young New York couple are enduring the lengthy visit of a mildly obnoxious British houseguest. At a party, the three meet a windy Texas businessman, "a States' Righter, a purchaser of Congressmen, a pillar of reaction," who entrances them all with his blunt, crude power. His vulgarity finally puts the carping Englishman on the defensive; and in his quasi-capitulation, before so much "gas," to America's "hideous vigor," he enters into a kind of comradeship at last with his hosts.

"Incest" begins with the description of a titillating dream that

Lee, a young husband, relates to his wife at supper; and it ends with him asleep and dreaming again. In between, he plays with his spoiled baby daughter while his exhausted wife rests; and he manages to lull the child to sleep with a bedtime story. As the title suggests, the story probes the complexity of a marriage involvement from the male perspective. In a sense, Lee is married not just to his wife but to her aggressive mother, whom she resembles, and also to his demanding child. The dream of the other woman, then, illustrates the familiar wish-fulfillment of basic Freudianism; but it also shows the husband's acceptance of his actual situation. In the end of the dream, he finds himself washing the mysterious blonde girl with a garden hose. She could be his daughter grown up, his secret ideal woman, his mother-in-law, or all three merged. In any case, "the task, like rinsing an automobile, was more absorbing than pleasant or unpleasant"; and such a reaction, Updike would say, is the reality of most of our experiences.

In "Intercession," Paul, the golf duffer, meets a lonely and insulting teenage boy on a Connecticut green. Exasperated by the boy's behavior, Paul does not see that it is a clumsy way of begging for companionship; and, instead of giving him the aid he needs, Paul challenges him to a round of golf for money. The boy refuses and goes away; Paul quits his playing and heads for his car, vaguely aware of failure but not of his central role in it.

In "The Alligators," which returns to the Olinger setting, Joan Edison is the new girl from Baltimore who enters the Olinger fifth grade in mid-semester. The class taunts her about her city ways; but Charlie (the protagonist), although he takes part in the persecution, secretly loves her and determines to confess it to her and become her champion against his classmates' torment. But, by the time he is ready to make his move, Joan has become "queen of the class." Charlie, an only child, has misinterpreted the strange manifestations of adolescent affection; he understands too late that the others all along teased her to make her one of them. As the eternal outsider, Charlie does not comprehend the rites of initiation; and, because he is so young, his alienation is all the more pitiful.

CHAPTER 2

The Poorhouse Fair:
The Godless City of God

> No windows intrude real light
> into this temple of shades.
> —from "Movie House"

I *The Shape of a First Novel*

THE POORHOUSE FAIR is the story of life in one sterile corner of the future welfare state: among the inhabitants and administrators of a New Jersey old people's home. But the novel in its mythical leanings is also an ironic portrayal of the realized modern City of God, ironic in that the new order has been achieved mainly by men of fervent social vision who long ago (from the vantage point of the novel) removed God from their universe and replaced him with the ideal of the perfect state. Doubly ironic, then, is that—within the institution of the old people's home, where all is tidiness and comfort and where all apparent needs are satisfied—the "senior citizens" of the model state are dissatisfied and await their deaths with the static boredom of those from whom science has taken away the hope of immortality. That elemental dissatisfaction excites the eruption of basic instincts which forms the incongruous climax of the novel.

The book has many of the earmarks of a *tour de force*. A novel about the aged, largely and convincingly from the perspective of the aged, it was written by a twenty-six-year-old young man. It dares to project itself into the future for time and setting—usually the domain of science fiction—and yet it maintains an essentially realistic tone. A first novel, it shows almost no signs of apprenticeship; instead, it is technically near-perfect. Its language reveals a studied lavishness that runs

31

counter to both the Hemingway and Faulkner prose traditions, but it convinces precisely through the virtuosity and discipline of idiom and image. The unique spatial and temporal setting, the strategy of perspective, the tension of age discrepancy in characterization, the subtle dimensionality of nearly plotless action, and the elaboration of language fuse to embody and to project the irony of the godless-City-of-God myth that provides, in turn, the thematic profundity of the story.

The Poorhouse Fair is a relatively short, three-part novel fashioned out of over forty cunningly blended vignettes. The events of the story transpire from morning to evening of a single day—the day traditionally set aside in late spring for the aged wards of the state to display outdoors and to sell to the public the quilts, the hand-carvings, and other wares they have made throughout the year for this event. In the first part, the old people casually prepare for the fair, setting up booths and stringing colored lights in spite of the threat of imminent rain; and their aimless busyness is interrupted only by such minor excitements as the appearance of a horribly crippled cat on the poorhome grounds and the arrival of the soft-drink truck bringing refreshments for the day. The young driver, bedeviled by some of the old men, backs his truck into the poorhome wall, demolishing a sizable section of it. At that moment, the rain begins to fall; and the old people disappear into the house for lunch.

The second part is dominated by the sitting-room discussion that occurs among various aged inhabitants and that is then interrupted and dominated by the prefect of the home. Since the rain appears to have ruined the plans for the fair, some of the old people gather after lunch in the sitting room to pass the time conversing and reading. The interchange begins with political reminiscences by old Hook, a ninety-year-old ex-schoolteacher who is the unacknowledged leader of the inhabitants. Conner, the prefect, who makes an unprecedented and not very welcome entry midway in the conversation, compulsively shifts the talk to the level of a political-religious argument.

Against Conner's own better judgment, he systematically destroys whatever religious faith and hope for immortality may have survived in the old people, substituting for them his own belief in the perfectibility of the socialized welfare state. In particular, he attempts to back old Hook into an intellectual corner and manages at least partially to shake the old man's trust in a benevolent natural universe. As the controversy becomes embarrassing, the antagonists are interrupted by the news that part of the band engaged to play at the fair has arrived in spite of the rain. Conner arranges to have the musicians play indoors for the inhabitants. Later in the afternoon the rain stops, and the old people plan to hold the fair after all.

The third part introduces an abrupt, brief, and violent action—the only action to speak of in the whole novel. With his obsession for order, Conner has instructed the old people to help him repair the damaged wall on the poorhouse grounds before the fair begins. While they are carrying stones to mend the damage, Gregg, a malicious old man who is slightly drunk at the moment, purposely throws a stone at the prefect and hits him on the leg, then another that strikes him in the back. Conner, both puzzled and frightened, begins a nervous retreat. Like excited savages, some other old people join Gregg in following Conner and pelting him with stones and dirt. The attack ceases as suddenly as it began; Conner has not been hurt, only humiliated. Hook has not participated in the stoning (in fact, he is too near-sighted to comprehend what is happening until it is over), yet later he is accused by Conner of instigating the attack and is insulted by the prefect and by his young aid.

The rest of the novel treats the fair itself, as various visitors mingle with the old people and as a sense of the inter-involvement of unrelated persons develops. The concluding vignette has old Hook waking up in the night following the fair, troubled by the vague feeling that there is something he must tell Conner, but what it is he cannot recall.

II *Autobiography and Fiction*

The poorhouse itself figures in Updike's own adolescent past. In "The Dogwood Tree: A Boyhood," which recalls his Pennsylvania childhood home, Updike writes: "The town was fringed with things that appeared awesome and ominous and fantastic to a boy. At the end of our street there was the County Home— an immense yellow poorhouse, set among the wide orchards and lawns, surrounded by a sandstone wall that was low enough on one side for a child to climb easily, but that on the other side offered a drop of twenty or thirty feet, enough to kill you

if you fell."[1] In retrospect, Updike sees the hollow in which
the poorhouse stood from a kind of Dantean perspective that
indicates the powerful impression its presence must have made
upon him; he describes it as "a dreadful pit of space congruent
with the pit of time into which the old people (who could be
seen circling silently in the shade of the trees whose very tops
were below my feet) had been plunged by some mystery that
would never touch me."[2]

In Updike's childhood memory, apparently, one finds the
experiential core of *The Poorhouse Fair*. The childish
fascination with the incomprehensible fact of death becomes the
creative impetus for the young artist who describes life on the
verge of its encounter with death. The sensation of Limbo that
held the boy (at least in retrospect) achieves necessary articula-
tion, then intellectual transformation, in the ironic City-of-God
vision of the adult novelist. Such transformation of personal past
into problematical fiction is characteristic of Updike's novelistic
strategy. His novels and stories sometimes depend upon autobiographical experience, and he has not at all attempted to con-
ceal that relationship from his audience. To the contrary, the
candid descriptions of childhood and youth in the "First Person
Singular" recollections of *Assorted Prose* allow the casual reader
to mark the similarities. Of particular interest is not that the
fiction provides insights into Updike's personal past but that he
has so insistently and skillfully translated his own background
into the compelling universalities of the novel and short story.

Certainly, all novelists draw in some degree from a personal,
historical past; but Updike persistently plumbs his past, constantly produces new variations upon a few key experiences,
and creates dramatized meanings for the present out of those
soundings. The poorhouse of Updike's boyhood is one of those
tangible realities that he mythologizes for the present. In terms
of the literal exploitation of setting, for whatever the information may be worth, the County Home on the edge of Shillington,
Pennsylvania, the town of Updike's birth, becomes in the novel
The Diamond County Home for the Aged on the outskirts of
the fictional Andrews, New Jersey. Just as Shillington is a
small-town satellite of the city of Reading, Pennsylvania, the
village of Andrews in the novel looks to nearby Trenton for
civic and state leadership. The depictions of buildings and
grounds of the real and fictional poorhouses are also similar. One

obvious reason, then, for the reader's acceptance of the strong sense of locale in *The Poorhouse Fair* is that Updike is able to project concrete memory into future setting and thereby to render that future familiar.

III   *The Futurist Setting*

The projection of the fictional time into the future, despite all of the possible overtones of science-fiction sensationalism, is accomplished without ostentation and for the artistic purpose of making viable the criticism of the welfare state. Actual dates are never mentioned; the year seems to be about 1975, but that is only deduced from off-handed bits of information. Otherwise, the aura of the future is established throughout the novel by occasional descriptions of ultra-modern technical devices and of political and social situations. Automobiles are "run by almost pure automation"; increasing longevity is making the welfare state itself more and more necessary; and race problems have disappeared: "Dark-skinned people dominated the arts and popular culture; intermarriage was fashionable, psychologists encouraged it; the color bar had quite melted."

Above all, international political and social conditions are changing radically according to what Updike introduces as the "well-publicized physical theory of entropia, the tendency of the universe toward eventual homogeneity, each fleck of energy settled in seventy cubic miles of otherwise vacant space. This end was inevitable, no new cause for heterogeneity being, without supernaturalism, conceivable." He speaks familiarly of the Americas as constituting "the Free Hemisphere" and as co-existing through "the London Pacts" with "the Eurasian Soviet" in an enervating stalemate. A President Lowenstein is chief of state, perhaps a playful allusion to the benevolent Eisenhower image (Eisenhower was in office at the time of the novel's composition), based on the Teutonic echoes in both names, and also a hint at the phenomenon of a Jewish president, as the associations of the name Lowenstein might suggest.

In describing the future, Updike runs the risk of all would-be prophets—that of having his vision checked by history as time catches up with his projection. Already it seems apparent that Updike has anticipated too much too soon; changes in the novel occur much more rapidly than they are actually taking place in society. For example, when Americans are described as a people "who had never fought a war that was not a holy war, and never lost one once begun," many United States citizens of the 1970's would disagree, the sardonic tone of the sentence notwithstanding. But such fiction need not be evaluated in terms of its detailed historical accuracy, only in terms of the efficacy of the use of the future as a metaphor of the present. Like most serious futuristic novels (Aldous Huxley's *Brave New World*; George Orwell's *1984*), *The Poorhouse Fair* is prophetic not in the sense of literal prognostication but as it warns against dangerous contemporary trends by envisaging the fearful excesses of their unchecked fulfillment. To Updike's credit, his first novel does not degenerate into social-political propaganda (unlike Huxley and Orwell); instead, it integrates the ironic utopian vision into its total purpose and accomplishment.

IV *Time and Space*

The elapsed time of the narrative is only twelve to perhaps fifteen hours, but these hours are packed so full of diverse action and shared from so many perspectives that one feels a true dimension of temporal scope and depth, of time passing and time experienced—both the chronological and existential aspects of time. The narrow framework of time is expanded as well through repeated backward glances. As one would expect among the aged, their significant thoughts in *The Poorhouse Fair* are mainly memories; the past for them is more vital and more actual than the present. As a result, the time structure of the novel could be compared to a pyramid, of which the apex, representing the immediate present of the narrative, rises out of the broad base of recollection and reminiscence that ranges all the way back to Hook's hazy memories of the late nineteenth century and then—up the pyramid—through the twentieth century to the lucidity of the disillusioning modern focus. Updike creates the effect of temporal depth primarily by giving his characters over to their nostalgic musings. Instead of providing objective descriptions of the past from an omniscient point of view, Updike places his characters in immediate situations that stimulate the aged memory and then allows the individual consciousness to take over; he has his old people move back and forth easily in their thoughts over a half-century and more of activity; and, through that technique, the basic framework of fifteen hours convincingly absorbs literally lifetimes of experience.

A similar twofold intensification of spatial setting develops in the novel. The actual narrative remains steadily anchored in the physical environs of the poorhome itself; no action takes place anywhere else, yet the constant variation of happenings in the house and on the grounds and the sheer rapid shifting of scenery within the circumference of the home assure sustained reader involvement. Then, as in the temporal dimension, the geographical setting (though not as thoroughly) expands through the memory. The aged inhabitants are constantly revitalizing old times in their minds, and they thereby revive also the old associations of place.

Hook particularly envisions his former Pennsylvania home that lies beyond the Delaware River, and in his musing he provides the novel with a certain longing for a desirable "beyond" that is physically based but, at the same time, is a state of mind. Conner acts as an illustration of the inverted process. Instead of visualizing the idealized past, Conner pictures the achieved utopia of the future for himself in graphic terms: "grown men and women, lightly clad, playing, on the brilliant sand of a seashore, children's games. . . . triangles and rhomboids flashingly formed by the intersection of legs and torsos scissoring in sport, and the modulated angles of nude thoracic regions, brown breasts leaning one against another, among scarves of everlasting cloth, beneath the sun." Conner's vision has no locale: it is the baseless dream of a spiritually orphaned idealist.

V *Sensuous Image and Extravagant Metaphor*

Updike's exercises in the use of time and space should not cause one to overlook another talent: his ability to compose striking physical descriptions, both in terms of literal phenomena and elaborate metaphor, the supplied sensuousness of spectacle as well as the imaginative synthesis of discrete images. When Buddy, the prefect's young aid, shoots the crippled cat, for instance, the following portrayal, with its quick emphasis on the visual, tactile, olfactory senses, is deftly sketched: "The animal dropped without a shudder. Buddy snapped back the bolt; the dainty gold cartridge spun away, and the gun exhaled a faint acrid perfume. . . . Going up to the slack body he insolently toed it over, annoyed not to see a bullet-hole in the skull. Chips of wood adhered to the pale fluff of the long belly. The bullet had entered the chin and passed through to the heart."

However adept Updike may be at creating the sensuous image, his stock in trade is the extravagant metaphor. His elegant control of the delicate tension between the tangible and the fanciful allows him to rely on the poetically wrought metaphoric analogy to carry the mood and tone (the emotional and intellectual temper) of his story. In the first part of *The Poorhouse Fair*, one finds a description of the doctor's eyes: "his green irises rode a boat of milk, under a white sky. Thus his eyes were targets." In Part II, when the blind Elizabeth Heinemann speaks: "her vowels were of different distinct colors, the consonants like leading in a window of stained glass." At the end of the novel, as two town boys are watching their girl friends parade naked in the shine of the automobile headlights, this subtly phallic description appears: "Above, the stars were not specks but needles of light suspended point downward in a black depth of stiff jelly."

In this approach to the depiction of spatial setting, through the elaborate metaphor, Updike demonstrates his departure from the dominant traditions of twentieth-century American fiction. It is true that he follows the Naturalistic mode now and again, but he seldom bothers with the transparent symbolic ciphers that our post-Naturalists have delighted in. Instead, he approximates in fiction the old-fashioned but often strangely new designs and effects of the Metaphysical poets. He economizes on the actual presentation of setting and he avoids the detailed and exhaustive effort of the Naturalists, but he still achieves the desired mood and tone in his settings through the evocative quality of his metaphors. Combined with the exploitation of spectacle, the use of extravagant metaphor—seldom quite a full-blown conceit—gives Updike's settings a fusion of realism and artifice that is unique in our age.

And those settings, in turn, support perfectly the irony of the godless City of God. From the innocence of the "pre-Creational landscape" of Elizabeth's sightless eyes and from Conner's "Michelangelesque mural" of the heavens, the overtones of pristine purity are sounded that fade into the void of hollow achievement. Men have at last pushed their knowledge far enough to overcome the Fall; but the price they pay, in becom-

ing like God, is the loss of God himself—and the perfect City
waits for vacant blessings under blank skies.

VI *The Non-Protagonist Strategy*

The two persons most attentively followed throughout the
narrative are Hook and Conner; and the antithesis that they form
is the working, thematic antithesis of the novel. Hook represents
the outmoded generation with its lingering absolute spiritual
values, a waning but necessary belief in the supernatural and in
the dignity of man's individuality. Conner, in contrast, is of the
new scientific humanist breed; he believes only in the empiri-
cally established and in the technologically possible. Skeptical
of human nature itself, he preaches the coming perfection of
machinery and bureaucracy but not of the human spirit. The
sitting-room debate in Part II draws the lines between them
with clarity and shows the impossibility of reconciliation. Hook
worships a benevolent Creator who still guides the universe;
and he argues eloquently, if archaically, for the fact of his existence. The name of Conner's god is Accident, and from that concept is derived his low estimate of humanity.

But neither Hook or Conner is, in the usual sense, the protagonist. The problem is not that the novel celebrates a non-
hero or an anti-hero of the variety which inhabits much contemporary fiction (Harry Angstrom is one in *Rabbit, Run*) but
that one discovers in *The Poorhouse Fair* no protagonist at all.
How has Updike achieved this anomaly? One answer lies
in the vignette quality of the book. The vignette by nature
stresses graceful design rather than a probing character analysis,
let alone psychoanalysis. *The Poorhouse Fair*, as a flowing
sequence of vignettes, depends, therefore, upon the gradual
accumulation of seemingly unimportant details for its effect
instead of upon forthright and dramatic personality confrontations. It is admittedly a risky way of composing fiction; the
danger always exists that the absence of a strong central character will also negate reader involvement—that traditionally vital
element of identification or vicarious experiencing (or with
the anti-hero, a perverse fascination) that draws the reader to
the novel. But Updike has taken that chance and succeeded.
One recognizes and accepts the truth of his total fictional
environment in a strangely unmediated manner, for it emerges

directly instead of through this or that character as mouthpiece or even as symbol.

The reader, in other words, becomes the protagonist in Updike's novel, although not in the sense of the *nouveau roman* reader participation, where the reader must solve compositional puzzles; Updike does the basic work himself, just as he must finally provide the culminating point of view. Even though Updike's theme is social and moral, he has written an artistic novel that stands or falls not on the power of message but on the strength of form. Whether or not this kind of fiction is more or less ambitious than another kind, it is infinitely more difficult to create and still maintain a more than precocious and esoteric appeal.

Updike's will to experiment is not the only reason for the strategy of the hero-less story: the theme itself happens to function best without a protagonist. In the new welfare state, homogeneity is the byword; therefore, a strongly individualistic, colorful hero or even anti-hero would be out of place. Where some sort of focus is necessary for purposes of contrast, Hook and Conner provide it. Hook (and most of the other old people) in his helpless, harmless disagreement with the smothering sameness of the accomplished society, and Conner in his flaccid compliance are the best possible substitutes for actual protagonists. The weak old man and the state's flunky are accented enough to project negatively the ironic theme but not enough emphasized to dominate the novel. The City achieves perfection at the cost not only of God but also of humanity; and its saints, therefore, must merge with the scenery.

VII   *Action and Substance*

Since Updike has not intended to write an action novel, the orthodox critical vocabulary including *plot, suspense, climax, resolution,* does not apply in the usual sense. The vignette nature of the novel already pre-empts the possibility of strong central action, but more important is the ironic vision that Updike has in mind: nothing happens in the novel because nothing happens in the realized City of God. The key word in *The Poorhouse Fair* is boredom: Conner is bored, the inmates are bored, society outside is bored; and, if the inmates are the least bored, it is because they have the relative richness of pre-utopian memories to dwell upon. In the state where homogeneity is the ideal, little conflict can exist. Where technological perfection is close at hand, there can be little anticipation, little chance of climactic action. The chief irony of the secular utopian dream is that, once it is actualized, it turns deadly and ruins its creators not through demonic execution but through sheer tedium. The lotus-eaters have subverted the space age.

Against this background, then, the single climactic action that transpires, the stoning of Conner, assumes greater meaning. The scene becomes a last desperate, pitiful gesture of defiance against the inevitable victory of the technological generation; and Updike's imagery evokes such an interpretation. The vignette for a moment becomes uncharacteristically laden with near-Expressionistic symbolism. Conner, the exacting, efficient agent of the new generation, demands order; the damaged wall around the poorhouse must be rebuilt for appearances' sake, so that visitors to the fair will not receive a bad impression. The old, male inmates are ordered to repair it. They look and function like primitives, with stooped shoulders and long-hanging arms, as they clumsily and slowly handle the heavy rocks. An instinctual savagery erupts among them, one strangely incongruous with the civilized super-society which cares for them and which Conner represents. Like wild animals sensing fear in their prey, the old men are excited by Conner's manner into attacking him.

The onslaught, of course, is as ineffectual as it is brief; Conner cannot be seriously hurt by the stones that the old men throw. What counts, literally and symbolically, is the spirit of the action. The attack by the aged is simultaneously brutal and hopelessly weak, a final wild protest by the last vitally *human* generation before life succumbs to the impersonal, collectivist monotony of the future. Cursing, screaming, and throwing earth, joined by the old women cackling obscenities, the old men of the old era have their final ecstatic moment. Before the incident is over they are laughing, ridiculing Conner and amused, apparently, at the absurdity of their own actions.

Paradoxically, the most positive note of the novel may be in that violent, primitive action, if one wishes to understand it as a sign that, beneath the hypnotic sameness of the utopian civilization, a disruptive quality still lurks. There may be a crack in the wall that surrounds the modern City of God, through which persons may escape into a wilderness of potential bestiality where life is tragically imperfect but where one can at least still find an individual identity.

VIII   *Language and Substance*

All discussion about Updike as a literary artist arrives sooner or later at his use of language. As prolific essayist and reviewer and as novelist, short-story writer, and poet, Updike has consistently displayed versatility in three areas: discursive, analytical prose; narrative fiction; and the image, metaphor, and rhythm of verse. Because his employment of language has always been spectacular in these three areas, he is regularly praised or damned for what his language does or does not accomplish. Part of the condemnation very likely involves guilt by association; Updike's tenure with *The New Yorker* (he has contributed to it in all three capacities, as critic-essayist, short story writer, and poet, both as a staff member and as independent author) has opened him to suspicion of sharing and perpetuating the image of glibness and sophisticated but superficial cleverness that marks the magazine. Regarding the majority of his poems and a good part of his essays, such as those that constituted "The Talk of the Town" column, the charge may be true: the pieces are elegant, knowledgeable, often playful, and easily forgotten—exactly what they are supposed to be. Whether or not one wants to consider Updike's *New Yorker* years his apprenticeship or not, he was hardly writing for posterity at the time but was being entertaining or casually informative. Apart from the lack of serious purpose or the absence of depth, the language of his verse and prose of that period is, if anything, remarkable for its consistency of polish and urbane correctness—in other words for its creation of wit in an extension of the eighteenth-century sense; and it is unfair to fault him for a missing profundity.

Updike's creation of dialogue in *The Poorhouse Fair* is superb; he has a good ear, one in tune with the modulations of the American voice: the lyric tones of the visionary, the antiquated echoes of the retired educator, the worried speculations of the middle-class wage-earner and his spouse, the inane mouthings of the prejudiced, the reflective vulgarities of the deprived and depraved are all notes on the novel's resonant scale.

It is almost refreshing to find an occasional awkward passage in Updike's fiction. He overextends himself, for instance, in the following sentence about Conner: "And the aura of holiday . . . infected him, and he began the flights of stairs, but not so suddenly Buddy did not communicate, through the simple pink oval of his face caught in the corner of Conner's eye as he seized the doorknob, amazement." The marooned word "amazement" following the long modifying clause produces an effect like Mark Twain speaking German. But such failings are extremely rare in Updike; when they do occur, they are all the more obvious against the backdrop of general excellence, but they are always compensated for by scores of superior metaphoric designs. When Conner pronounces a "no" to the question of a potential heaven on earth for the old people, Updike writes, "The word hung huge in the living room, the 'o' a hole that let in the cold of the void." It is Updike's power of words that creates in this novel a believable world out of the stuff of negation.

IX Sensibility and Compassion

In a review of a Muriel Spark novel, Updike wrote:

Our [American] novels tend to be about education rather than products of it; they are soul-searching rather than worldly-wise. English fiction, for all the social and philosophical earthquakes since Chaucer, continues to aspire, with the serenity of a treatise, to a certain dispassionate elevation above the human scene. Hence its greater gaiety and ease of contrivance, its (on the whole) superior finish, and its flattering air of speaking to the reader who, himself presumably educated, may be spared the obvious. But in the last analysis human experience is mired in a solipsism to which America's strenuous confessional exercises are faithful, and authors who rise above the accidents of autobiography are at the mercy of the accidents of knowledgeability.[3]

This quotation has relevance for Updike himself as a novelist, for he is one of those few American writers who has risen above the accident of autobiography and who has *chosen* to use autobiography with a degree of knowledgeability that at least matches his British contemporaries. *The Poorhouse Fair*, in fact, is more "worldly-wise" than "soul-searching," and it also displays the dispassionate quality and "superior finish" that Updike attributes to English fiction.

But Updike is not a victim of his style. His fiction is marked by a certain humility which may or may not be an American virtue and for which there exists no satisfactory term in the literary critical vocabulary. Whether it is the Pennsylvania Dutch honesty combined with the Harvard sophistication or some other chemistry that gives Updike his artistic singularity, his fiction is never snobbish or condescending. Nor, in spite of the total transformation of the autobiographical backgrounds, is Updike ever a *poseur*. One gets the impression, even in the first novel, of a professional who knows thoroughly what he is doing and who, therefore, has no need of disguises—nothing like the self-indulgent mysticism of Salinger, for instance, or the new-journalistic voices of Mailer.

What removes the chill from the ironic and cynical *The Poorhouse Fair* is the presence of compassion—a compassion that is the result of humility and talent—that renders the most negative situation affirmative by a sympathetic study of even the unlovable characters. That trait becomes even more marked in the following novels and stories, and it has led to the frequent charge that Updike wastes his craft by expending it on worthless types. But he seeks only to understand the modern world by comprehending the variations of the human species. He does not therefore write "confessional exercises" in the American tradition but artistic confession in the Goethean sense—as a compassionate record of mankind's struggles for meaning and being, which, constituted as it is from autobiography and knowledgeability, is more convincing than the American legacy alone.

The prefatory quotation to *The Poorhouse Fair* is the conclusion of an apocalyptic prophecy attributed by Luke the Evangelist to Jesus: "If they do this when the wood is green, what will happen when the wood is dry?" The question, of course, is appropriate to the theme of the generations in the novel: maturity does not necessarily bring wisdom and righteousness. Applied to Updike's ironic utopia, it means, simply, that the perfection of technological achievement is not the solution to most human ills. Jesus' words are spoken as part of an eschatological vision that anticipates the advent of the Kingdom of God with all its cataclysmic trappings. But in *The Poorhouse Fair* one sees that the cataclysm has not arrived and never will. This novel about the future, in a final irony, compels one to acknowledge that there is no future for a humanity that delimits itself by a surrender to officialdom and to the machine. The price of perfection is no less than the human spirit itself.

CHAPTER 3

Rabbit, Run:
The Quest for a Vanished Grail

How promiscuous is
the world of appearances!
—from "Suburban Madrigal"

I *Morality in Motion*

THE POORHOUSE FAIR is an achievement of tightly controlled microcosmic focus, an amazing display of form from a relatively inexperienced writer. *Rabbit, Run* maintains the discipline, accelerates the power, broadens the scope, and popularizes the interest. It is extremely sensual, clinically sexual, cynically middle-class, and insistently moral. A few book reviewers have implied that Updike composed his second novel as a purposely sensational shocker to capture the American mass audience, but Updike sacrifices no integrity whatsoever in *Rabbit, Run*. It is not to his career at all what *Sanctuary*, say, was to Faulkner's. In the relaxing of censorship standards and in the ensuing flood of explicitly sexual novels that have appeared since the publication of *Rabbit, Run* in 1960, Updike's book has largely lost its capacity for shock, and it can now be appraised much more objectively in terms of its artistic qualities.

The novel is not deficient in the fictional risks that one learns to expect from Updike. In *The Poorhouse Fair*, Updike moves dangerously close to gimmickry in depicting a proximate science-fiction future; in *Rabbit, Run*, he displays a similar fascination with time that leads him into a more difficult experiment. He composes the whole novel in the historical present to provide a precarious dramatic immediacy—a short story technique that functions very well in this long narrative.

45

In addition, if *The Poorhouse Fair* is a *tour de force* of sorts as the accomplishment of a young man composing a sensitive and empathetic novel about the aged, *Rabbit, Run* is no less so as a story that runs along archetypal heroic lines, yet is utterly devoid of heroic characters and situations. Updike gives himself practically nothing to create from: not a colorful setting but just a common, conventional, slightly squalid Pennsylvania suburban town; not even an anti-hero but just a non-hero with still less potential for tragedy than Arthur Miller's salesman.

The enveloping ironic myth in *The Poorhouse Fair* is the godless City of God; one could call the archetype of *Rabbit, Run* the futile quest for the nonexistent Holy Grail. Although Updike never mentions it as such, the futile quest is present in the sheer nervous movement, in the ceaseless search of the protagonist for a Something that he himself cannot identify. The non-hero runs compulsively but aimlessly through an industrialized wasteland, dogged by a lust that distorts his relationships with all others but that at least blots out the pain of the archetypal wound: the deadly boredom, almost unbearable, of daily life. Even the Chapel Perilous does not offer a decisive experience but instead, as the edifice of modern Protestantism, becomes a kind of spiritual spa which protects the best-kept secret: that men are all, behind their conditioned reflexes, nonbelievers; and that the quest has no goal.[1]

Rabbit, Run, like *The Poorhouse Fair*, is divided into three sections: two equally long initial and middle parts and a short climactic conclusion. Unlike the first novel, it is composed not of brief vignettes but of about twenty scenes of varying length, some extending to as much as thirty-five pages (the first one) and others of only a single paragraph. The opening scene shows the central character, Harry "Rabbit" Angstrom, twenty-six-year-old ex-basketball star of Mt. Judge High, as he pauses on his way home from work for a game of alley basketball with some half-willing teenagers. Arriving home late to Janice, his pregnant, tippling, and TV-entranced wife, he is overcome by disgust as he considers how shallow and false his daily life has become.

He leaves with no explanation and on impulse spends the night driving his car in the direction of the United States southland, teased by romantic visions of an easy life there.

He gets as far as West Virginia, turns around, and returns during the early morning through eastern Pennsylvania to Mt. Judge—not to his home but to the apartment of Tothero, his old high school coach. Tothero takes him in; that evening on a double date, Rabbit meets Ruth Leonard, a prostitute, achieves an immediate sexual rapport with her, and moves into her apartment. The rest of the section treats the growing affair between Ruth and Rabbit and the efforts of Eccles, the young Episcopalian minister, to make Rabbit face the responsibility of his marriage.

The second section resumes the narrative two months later. Rabbit is still living with Ruth; Janice with their small son has moved into her parents' home and is waiting to have her baby. In two major scenes from the section, the point of view, which has been exclusively Rabbit's, shifts briefly to Eccles and his painful discussions with the parents of Rabbit and Janice, then to Ruth's stream-of-consciousness musings about her un-witting slide into prostitution. The story then moves back to Rabbit. On a double date with Ruth and another couple, he learns details of Ruth's former sex life that anger him; and that night he asks her to perform fellatio, a humiliating act for her that undermines whatever genuine love may have been between them.

The same night he learns that Janice is in labor, rushes full of guilt and contrition to the hospital, and resolves to redeem their marriage. He lives at home with Nelson their son while Janice recovers; when she returns, they share a satisfying life for nine days. Then on a Sunday he attends the Episcopalian service and returns home aroused by a suggestive post-church encounter with Lucy Eccles, the minister's young wife. He tries awkwardly to make love with Janice that afternoon; when she rejects him, he leaves and stays away all night. Janice, in despair, drinks herself into a near stupor; on Monday, the next day, she inadvertently drowns their new baby daughter while bathing her.

In the third and final section, Rabbit learns from Eccles of the death of his daughter and returns to Janice and his in-laws. They prepare numbly for the funeral on Tuesday afternoon. After the chapel service and in the cemetery, Rabbit has an ecstatic, reconciliatory religious experience that turns into a breakdown after the burial. He suddenly tells the horri-fied mourners that the baby's death was not his fault and, in the same breath, tries to console his wife. Then he runs away with

Eccles in pursuit. Eccles cannot catch him. That evening Rabbit slips back into town and goes to Ruth's apartment. He learns from Ruth that she is pregnant with his child. When he cannot bring himself to consider a divorce from Janice, Ruth throws him out. The novel ends with Rabbit's running aimlessly and in panic through the night.

II *Images of the Non-Hero*

The complexity of Harry Angstrom's personality, which is metaphoric of the complexity of experienced reality, is apparent in the nature and objects of his quest. The ironic search for the nonexistent Grail may serve as the guiding myth, but the dimensions of his quest are, on the one hand, more primitive than that and, on the other, more specifically modern. The quest reaches into the reflexive, instinctual depths of his animal being, out into the social context, and blindly toward a spiritual realm that is barely conceivable in this skeptical age. Updike shapes image and scene to fashion, therefore, a novel that is a unique blend of the cerebral and the biological. Without exaggerating the protagonist's self-understanding (Rabbit is not stupid, but neither is he self-consciously perceptive), Updike develops, largely from the perspective of the central character, an acutely analytical study of personality.

In terms of the most obvious image, Updike prompts the reader to see in Harry the qualities, mainly liabilities, that his nickname implies. First, he looks something like a rabbit: "the breadth of white face, the pallor of his blue irises, and a nervous flutter under his brief nose as he stabs a cigarette into his mouth partially explain the nickname." Throughout the novel, such physical hints are dropped: "His upper lip nibbles back from his teeth in self-pleasure"; "Rabbit stealthily approaches his old home on the grass, hopping the little barberry hedge"; "Today was payday. Fingering so much lettuce strengthens his nerves"; "Rabbit hops up to Ruth's step and kisses her"; "Himself, he is not a water animal."

The implicit qualities are just as fitting. Harry, like his animal namesake, is mild in nature and openly harmless, even a frightened creature; but if he is allowed to roam unchecked, he can do damage through his constant and voracious appetites. In line with the ironic quest motif of the novel, he is always ready for flight, always poised to escape when life threatens him, and is indeed often on the run and in hiding. Even when secure, he is afflicted by a twitchiness, a nervous agitation that upsets those around him. More important, he shares the rabbit's reputation for reproduction; in a few month's time, he has impregnated two women and automatically considers women in terms of sexual encounter. The fundamental image thus fixes the dominant element of characterization in the novel: Rabbit is a dangerous man, and all the more so because of the deceptively bland façade; the reverse side of his good-naturedness is a fatal weakness of character, the inability to check his animal lusts and his visceral impulses that leads to pure irresponsibility.

A second image that gradually assumes an archetypal form is that of the modern sports hero. The nervous motion that marks the rabbit imagery is also part of the basketball game. Rabbit, a county basketball star eight years before the story begins, has difficulties because he has known adulation and success in his immaturity and has made them an impossible ideal for his adulthood. Basketball is not really a game for him but a model for existence. When, for example, he assesses his marriage against the feeling that basketball gave him, he finds it lacking. As he tries to explain to Eccles, "I once played a game real well. I really did. And after you're first-rate at something, no matter what, it kind of takes the kick out of being second-rate. And that little thing Janice and I had going, boy, it was really second-rate."

The rabbit image is appropriate for guiding the characterization in the novel, while the image of the basketball game directs the action. Therefore, it is not by accident that Updike begins *Rabbit, Run* with the alley basketball scene. Harry Angstrom, pushing his way into a casual teenagers' game, is nostalgically and pathetically trying to recapture the fame of his faded high school career. Only half-mindful of the resentment he fires in the outclassed boys, he loses himself briefly in the illusion of his past minor glory: Rabbit sees himself as an ex-hero. The whole novel, in a sense, is his restless, mindless necessity of trying to become all over again the county high scorer, the champion, the darling of the crowds.

Since basketball has been his model for life, life itself is ultimately just a game. Marriage, fatherhood, job, religion are all somehow play; he still believes in the platitudinous mouthings of his old coach ("the will to achieve," "giving our best") as the magic formulas for success—just as he heeds the banal preachings on television of Jimmy the Mouseketeer. Conversely, Rabbit's sporadic attempts to escape his marriage and his town and his shifting from job to job represent his desire to quit the game, to get off the court. His frustration and his resultant panic grow from the knowledge that he must keep on playing when the playing no longer produces sensual pleasure or egotistical satisfaction.

Rabbit is not, it should be emphasized, an anti-hero, Existentialist or otherwise. He is not a radical individualist asserting his total freedom as he challenges the mores of his society. Nor is he an ultimately lovable and forgivable picaresque rascal who disguises a stellar nature behind the scrapes that involve him. The anti-hero has qualities that society may not value, but they are at least of the kind that give him individuality and identity and that provoke unwilling admiration. Neither is Rabbit the rugged common man, unspectacular but "true-blue," of the American myth. He seems to have few attributes at all, certainly no heroic virtues. He is a weak-willed conformist, not a rebel. Irresponsible, undependable, and gutless, he is the quintessence of the non-hero. That Updike has not made him an entirely despicable man but has instead cast him in the ironic mold makes the portrayal all the more effective.

III   *The Quest*

The quest motif is not just behind the novel as the archetypal material but is handled implicitly as an important part of the thematic pattern. Once again the irony is central: the search has no direction, no goal, and no end; the Grail certainly has no objective existence; and Rabbit has defined it only vaguely. The quest, furthermore, has double dimensions in that it is always a flight away from something and a search for something else. Both the opening scene (after the basketball game) and the closing one exemplify the flight-search dimension. In Rabbit's initial night drive to West Virginia (a scene that is a fine fictional accomplishment by itself), he is escaping a suffocating marriage and chasing an impossibly romantic vision: "He wants to go south, down, down the map into orange groves and smoking rivers and barefoot women."

The trip is rife with ironic illusion and allusion, for he drives through such towns as Bird in Hand, Intercourse, and Paradise, Pennsylvania. He listens on the car radio to Connie Francis and Mel Torme torching their tributes to American pop erotica (the modern equivalent of the courtly love verse?), and he considers (as he is stimulated, of all things, by Wilmington, Delaware) the unique thrills of making love to a Du Pont woman. Rabbit is the modern knight roaming the countryside in his 1955 Ford, crooning "Ev, reebody loves the, cha cha cha"; and he ends alone, womanless, and lost in a backwoods lovers' lane. His journey is pathetic and sordid—pathetic, because the only adventures along the way are the cheap offerings of manufactured music, bad roadside food, and vicarious sex; sordid, because, of all the chivalric qualities, the only one that Rabbit seems to possess is the capacity for adultery. It is a revival of the cliché to remark that in all of this flight and search Rabbit is looking for himself, but it is true nevertheless. Yet when the half-drunk gas station attendant tells him, "The only way to get somewhere, you know, is to figure out where you're going before you go there" (shades of *Alice in Wonderland*), Rabbit is insulted. The tragedy—or the farce—of the novel is that he never learns. So, at the end of the story, having alienated absolutely everyone but the long-suffering Eccles, Rabbit is in flight once more as he tries to escape the chaos of himself through the sheer physicality of running.

One could no doubt make a case for the presence of the archetypal search behind most any novel that traces the wanderings of the spirit, if only for the reason that life itself, at least in Western culture, is a grand search for concepts of value which is then reflected in fiction. But Updike renders the mythic underpinnings of the quest unmistakably clear in his images of the Grail as its culmination. Rabbit himself in his dialogic joustings with Eccles returns time and again to oblique queries about this indefinable thing he is hunting. Trapped into thought by the young minister, Rabbit says inanely, "I *do* feel, I guess, that somewhere behind all this . . . there's something that wants me to find it." Eccles' retort is laconically to the point: "all vagrants think they're on a quest. At least at first." In their continuing encounters, the Grail becomes an algebraic "X" that substitutes for the missing element in Rabbit's marriage, in his sex life, and in his religion. While playing golf with the runaway husband (Eccles functions better

on the golf course than in the pulpit or pastorate), Eccles starts
a line of conversation that goes like this:

"Harry, . . . why have you left her? You're obviously deeply involved
with her."
"I *told* ja. There was this thing that wasn't there."
"What thing? Have you ever seen it? Are you sure it exists?"
. . . . "Well if you're not sure it exists don't ask me. It's right up
your alley. If you don't know nobody does."

Eccles does not know, as a matter of fact; for, apparently
trapped into the ministry by parental expectations (his father
was a clergyman before him), he is without a faith that he
can communicate. Compassion he has, but he cánnot pass that
on as a formula to a Rabbit who seeks the security of a simple
and infallible dogma. And yet, paraxodically, Rabbit senses what
he is after. Still on the golf course and arguing pointlessly with
Eccles, Rabbit hits a beautiful drive from the tee that fills him
with the emotional-esthetic purity of his basketball days. " 'That's
it!' he cries and, turning to Eccles with a smile of aggrandize-
ment, repeats, 'That's it!' " Eccles' last words before the feat have
been, significantly, "You don't care about right or wrong; you
worship nothing except your own worst instincts." Rabbit does
worship—at least trusts in—his own instincts; but such worship
is a reaction to a dominant Puritanism that dictated his religious
training and that still controls his environment.

For Rabbit and the romantic tradition he unwittingly adopts,
natural depravity yields to the potential divinity of one's own
being; and the old search for redemption becomes the romantic
search for the infinite. Both concepts fit perfectly the ironic
pattern of Rabbit's life as imaged in the Grail hunt; according
to the legend, only the pure in heart have hope of finding the
elusive Grail. Rabbit, for all of his perversity, incredibly sees
himself in terms of that purity, for he has been duped by the
hero reflex into believing his instincts, and they tell him consistently that what he feels good in doing must *be* good.

Rabbit often experiences remorse—he is still too much the
Puritan not to—but it fades in the exhilaration of instinctive
action. In the absorption of animated emotion, in the sublima-
tion of the spirit to the sensations of the flesh (Rabbit, like all
romantics, still accepts that dichotomy), he comes closest to the
fulfillment of the second concept: that reaching for the infinite

in order to satisfy some appetite or psychological need originating in the here-and-now. The ironic circularity is apparent: inspired by the grandness of his quest Rabbit is at last pitifully content to identify his Grail with the sex act, the athletic success, the ambiguous praise of a friend, so that, despite all his wandering, he ends up where he began.

The pathos of the novel that results from an application of the archetypal Grail-quest configuration lies in the melancholy revelation that Rabbit, despite his suffering, never becomes the initiate. At one point, it appears, however, that he will: living alone with little Nelson while Janice is recovering from the birth, Rabbit, willing to make a new start, "feels the truth: the thing that had left his life had left irrevocably; no search would recover it. No flight would reach it." But through the seductive ecstasy of an emotionalized religious experience at the graveyard ceremony he loses the truth that could ripen and mature him. When the others misunderstand the experience, he reverts to form—the form of the non-hero who does what is most natural for him: he runs. Because Rabbit has lived by his reflexes, he becomes, finally, no more than a reflex.

IV   *Oedipus in Pennsylvania*

It should be apparent from the discussion of the mythic patterns in *Rabbit, Run* that the major characters are not entirely normal people in normal situations. A young husband with an escape complex, a helpless wife, a prostitute in business since her early teens, and an unbelieving Christian clergyman are hardly examples of an emotionally healthy society. When one adds to these characters a high school coach turned sexual masochist, a come-hither pastor's wife, parents and in-laws in various stages of mutual antagonism, one has a catalogue of neuroses on hand that rivals Eugene O'Neill's finest collections. Yet Updike is not an enthusiastic psychologizer. He does not sully his novel by random dabblings in amateur analysis. The psychological dimension of Updike's characters is just one aspect of their human complexity. Unlike the fictionalized case histories of, say, D. H. Lawrence's sufferers in *Sons and Lovers,* or more recently, the single-minded addicts in James Purdy's absurd world, Updike's people are first believable people—and then they are people with problems that may or may not have psychoanalytical labels. The

density of their artistic composition makes them real; their flaws
and illnesses of personality make them approachable.

The inner parallel to Rabbit's mythic quest for the Grail is
his obsessive need for the ideal mother and lover. One hesitates
to revive once more the subject of the Oedipus complex, over-
worked as it has been in modern literature and in criticism since
the advent of Freudianism; but one need not really apologize for
its appearance in *Rabbit, Run*. Updike uses it with subtle vitality
as a unifying focal image that magnifies the motivations, the
desires, and the destinies of the protagonist and those who are
bound up in his existence.

Rabbit's *angst* (his surname contains the term) forces him to a
dual reaction that involves the two faces of the Oedipal dilemma.
He gropes toward the innocent past (life with the mother) and
fumbles with sex (life with the lover), and he unconsciously
strives to use both as security and anodyne. The backdrop of his
struggle is the void of his meaningless present which asserts itself
as boredom and as a paralysis of the will. Against that terrible
blank he draws security from the past as he attempts to return
to the womb; on the night of his daughter's birth, he even
sleeps in the foetal position. But the past, the prenatal home
in the womb, is also an anodyne as it offers the false hope of
vegetable comfort, just as the sex act invites to momentary forgetfulness through the consuming sensual pleasure of physical
indulgence.

Rabbit is the *son-sun* with all of the metaphysical connotations
of the pun, and the female characters are the satellites in orbit
around him: Janice; Ruth; his mother; Lucy Eccles; Mim, his
sister; and even old Mrs. Smith his employer, and Becky, his
fated baby. A good part of Rabbit's frustration is that he seeks
fulfillment of an ideal nearly as impossible to realize as his
vague religious search: he wants to find in one woman the
security of the mother and the excitement of the lover. His
society being what it is, he could feasibly find each in separate
women, but that will not do for Rabbit because he is tempera-
mentally monogamous, a family man at heart for all his rabbity
excursions. Here the connection between his hero neurosis on
the general level and his Oedipal problem on the particular one
becomes clear: his need to be loved by the crowd, which includes
the comfort and excitement of adulation, is but the broad
expression of what he desires in the marriage relationship. The

woman who accepts him in bed must not only pat him on the head but also dry his tears. He has been spoiled by his parents and his society into believing that a wife should exercise both functions for him, and he is disillusioned when reality proves otherwise.

His rejection of Janice, therefore, and the attraction of the prostitute Ruth are for him psychologically predictable. Janice is the high school love partner who, in growing up, has failed to mature as a mother; Ruth is the whore whose maternal qualities are almost stronger than the attraction of her promiscuity. Rabbit and Janice have never experienced anything approaching a genuine marriage relationship. The original rapport was sexual, beginning as a series of secret assignations in a girlfriend's bedroom and culminating in a hasty wedding when Janice's pregnancy became apparent. In a flashback, in one of Rabbit's reminiscences depicting such a premarital adventure, Updike foreshadows the inevitable dead end of the marriage not yet even planned. "Lying side by side on this other girl's bed, feeling lost, having done the final thing."

The recurring vision of Janice that Rabbit wants to recapture is not of his wife as mother but as the naked and eager lover, and that vision is based on one experience alone that catches Janice out of character. After the marriage, their sex life has degenerated, as if it needed the stimulus of the clandestine. Rabbit is caught with the sloppy, listless, and pregnant (now for the second time) ex-high school student; and all he can do about her is to hope pathetically (one notices the teenage idiom) "that tomorrow she'll be his girl again." Far from satisfying Rabbit's desires for a mother and a lover in one, Janice is no longer even the lover.

If Janice is neither, Ruth seems to hold the promise of becoming both. As a prostitute, she has the sexual sophistication that Janice lacks; but she also possesses the motherly nature and attributes that are alien to Rabbit's wife. She cooks very well and likes it; she keeps a clean apartment; she even takes a legitimate job to help support the two of them when Rabbit moves in with her. Above all, once Rabbit has cracked the toughness of her professional veneer, she caters to him with her maternal instincts and gives him the emotional protection he needs. It seems that to solve the predicament, Rabbit should divorce Janice and marry Ruth. He could do so, since Janice's parents are well-to-do and sympathetic and will care for her; moreover, Janice herself is resigned to the separation in her childish way. But Rabbit is much too entangled in the knots of his personality, too vacillating in his capricious sense of obligation, to carry through a divorce and a re-marriage. Instead he does—typically —nothing; and he loses Ruth.

Although Updike is not especially interested in probing Rabbit's past to indicate the root of his complex, he provides enough details of Rabbit's relations with his parents to show that his trouble began with them. The scene in which Eccles visits the senior Angstroms (an incident balanced by the discussion with Mrs. Springer, Janice's mother) places much of the blame on Rabbit's rearing. Mrs. Angstrom, the dominant parent, is the strong-willed wife whose bitterness at the weaker husband who has not fulfilled her expectations she sublimates into overlove for her son. In the conversation with the minister, she defends Harry ("Hassy," she still calls him, curiously like the German *Hase*—"rabbit"); but the husband condemns him. For her, Rabbit is the victim; and Janice is the manipulator who managed "to get herself pregnant so poor Hassy has to marry her when he could scarcely tuck his shirttail in." Her husband's reaction is quite the opposite: "He's become the worst kind of Brewer bum. If I could get my hands on him, Father, I'd try to thrash him if he killed me in the process." When the discussion deteriorates into mutual accusations about the parents' marriage, Eccles hears and sees enough to guess at the almost transparent causes for Rabbit's confusion: the "rumpus" scenes (as Rabbit's father euphemizes them) between the parents have had a cumulative and deleterious effect on the son.

The final lines of the psychological pattern in the family are drawn in as Eccles leaves. Rabbit's nineteen-year-old sister Mim comes in as the minister departs; he turns around from the street to see old Angstrom still standing there with his arm around his daughter. Electra complements Oedipus; the son's love of his mother is matched by the daughter's relation to her father. The difference in the two situations, as Eccles feels it, is that the father and daughter will endure, while the mother and son may fall, because of these subconscious sexual relationships. Appearances and patterns deceive: Mrs. Angstrom's love and her son's idealistic sensitivity make them vulnerable, whereas a built-in vulgarity of father and daughter renders them impervious to suffering. Mrs. Angstrom has at least given that gift to her son: the capacity for suffering, and it increases his humanity. His misfortune is that he cannot live his sorrow into tragedy and gain moral stature at the end.

V *The Revenge of Eros*

If the literary critical psychoanalyzing of Rabbit's predicament is so inconclusive, why should one bother with it? A reason is that it demonstrates how Updike, precisely by creating an abnormal figure, forces one to realize that the abnormal has become, paradoxically, the representative of the norm. John Barth, a contemporary of Updike with a similar power of fictional composition, has remarked that his task in writing the modern novel is to resolve apparent contradictions into paradox. Updike is doing the same thing. If paradox is what one finally arrives at, it is at least a category of logic that imposes a measure of order—this era's substitute for Classical and Christian order—upon chaos. And, if the psychological configurations help one to image the paradox, they serve their purpose.

A second reason, more specifically artistic, is that the psychologizing of character leads to a greater clarity regarding the total strategy of the novel. Rabbit's own movement is from reflexive action to an attempted self-understanding; although that attempt ends in failure, to trace it is to realize the fullness of troubled humanity that Updike's people contain. Rabbit's behavior as the Oedipal son-husband is actualized in his interrelations with his mother, his wife, and his mistress; but the other women in the story complete his pattern. Lucy Eccles is the most fascinating of these. Committed to a life of social respectability as a pastor's wife, she is actually a disciple of Freud who believes more in the power of instinctive sexuality than in transcendent divinity. She chafes under the restrictions that the parsonage placed upon her and finds an immediate attraction—even a perverse delight—in defining Rabbit upon their first meeting as a "primitive" husband and father—one utterly different from her own mate, the self-conscious, dutiful Jack Eccles. Rabbit sees her as a potential "lay" (in his own vulgar idiom), as the goal of a particularly interesting sexual adventure, since her social position is what it is (perhaps a substitute for the unattainable Du Pont girl?); but it is partially her fault that she affects him that way. Although her invitations to him appear more tantalizing to his over-stimulated imagination than they are really intended to be, the flirtatious overtones are there; and in one sense she is to blame for the fatal sequence of events in the last part of the novel.

After Rabbit attends Eccles' church, marking another stage in his rehabilitation as husband and father, Lucy asks him to walk her home. Her conversation is daring; she asks him in for coffee. When he takes the invitation too intimately, she is insulted; but the damage is done. "Whether spurned or misunderstood, Eccles' wife has jazzed him, and he reaches his apartment clever and cold with lust." When Janice, still convalescing from the birth of their daughter, will not make love with the aroused Rabbit, he deserts her again. She takes solace in her alcohol and, in a drunken accident, drowns the baby. Ironically, Lucy Eccles has a more destructive hand than anyone in frustrating her husband's own ego-salving game of redeeming Rabbit.

Rabbit exudes an erotic magnetism. He is a sexual animal, and women respond. There is a loving sensuality to nearly everything he does, from fondling a basketball to eyeing a blossoming school girl to stroking a sex partner; as a result, he lives in a state of excited anticipation that expends energy in the drive for satisfaction. One of the main artistic achievements of the novel is the manner in which Updike indirectly marks Rabbit's obsession: he depicts Rabbit as quite unable to confront any eligible woman except in terms of her sexual desirability. Rabbit's preoccupation with breasts and pudenda is a sign of his use of sex as security and anodyne. They are the parts that fire his *angst*-deadening lust, but they also suggest the womb and the infant nurture to which he longs to return: thus the strange double attraction that pregnant women exercise over him. His final expression of desire for Ruth is typical: "If he can just once more bury himself in her he knows he'll come up with his nerves all combed." Other nuances are frequent: Rabbit insists on washing Ruth's face before making love to her, but he wants to sleep cradled in her arm; when he sees his daughter for the first time behind the window of the hospital nursery, he also studies the nurse holding her; and when he sees his mother after the baby's death, at the funeral home, Updike describes it thus: "she steps toward him with reaching curved arms. 'Hassy, what have they done to you?' She asks this out loud and wraps him in a hug as if she would carry him back to the sky from which they have fallen."

In the final pages of the novel, all of Rabbit's women are somehow present. Janice, his mother, and Mim are at the cemetery; baby Becky has been buried; and, as he runs from the grave, he wonders about Lucy Eccles: would she have had him? And he finds himself at last back at Ruth's apartment. It is as if, at the end, persons and circumstance combine to overwhelm Rabbit with a surfeit of the figures of his sexual quest but in a manner that robs him of its goal, of the comfort and forgetfulness it should provide. Rabbit reaches the second circle of his private Inferno: appetite becomes nausea, security gives way to panic, and the sexual sinner is condemned to the incessant running and buffeting of Dante's carnal damned.

The sexual saturation of the novel is anything but an attempt at fictional sensationalism through an appeal to the salacious. Rabbit's immersion in sex is frightening and negatively instructive—instructive because his whole glandular existence is a contorted effort at discovering love. Ruth, the professional lover, clumsily states the ideal when she tries to tell Rabbit why she has slept around: "What *do* you do? You make love, you try to get close to somebody." One must *make* love, of course, because love is no longer naturally forthcoming in a world that demands pleasure without responsibility. Rabbit's attempt to use everybody for his truncated kind of affection (mirrored in his obsession for all varieties of women) becomes an obscene travesty of the unselfish, genuine spirit of love. It is not just that *Eros* crowds out *Agape*; *Eros* itself is wronged (thus the significance of the humiliating fellatio scene)—and *Eros* in the name of total love revenges itself upon the culprit. Over a decade later, in *Rabbit Redux*, Updike would reveal the intensity of that revenge.

CHAPTER 4

Pigeon Feathers:
The Design of Design

Claustrophobia attacks
us even in air.
—from "Earthworm"

I *The Reconstructive Memory*

PIGEON FEATHERS AND OTHER STORIES, Updike's second collection of short fiction (published in 1962), contains stories
that had appeared over the past three years (with the exception
of two brief sketches) in *The New Yorker*. A very uneven book,
it includes some of the poorest and some of the best fiction that
Updike has composed. The weakness of the inferior stories
derives from Updike's willingness to vary the use of mastered
forms with experiments in new directions; but, occasionally,
as in the sermon "Lifeguard" and in the final semi-autobiographi-
cal narrative in the collection, he succeeds with the new modes.
Some of the other stories, such as the epistolary "Dear Alexandros" and "Archangel," are notable only for their artifice.

In *The Same Door*, the thematic stress is on the unexpected
gifts of personal encounter; in *Pigeon Feathers*, the accent
shifts to the individual in greater spiritual isolation and in a
struggle to come to terms with the universe itself, even though
the context is the familiar round of ordinary events. In *The
Same Door*, the narrative strategy is to produce the cumulative
epiphany; in *Pigeon Feathers*, the evocative memory works more
often to re-quicken a significant moment from the past that
could lend meaning to the present. The farther Updike moves
from his own shaping past, it seems, the tighter he holds its
remnants.

These stories emphasize not only the spark of grace within

the ordinary worldly happenings but the existence and awareness of design in all human events and conditions. All fiction consists of design, of course, but *Pigeon Feathers* ventures a double concentration upon it. Updike employs design to talk about design. The artistic and thematic matrices are virtually identical; the language and meaning of fictive metaphor become one. The paradigm of names in "Walter Briggs," the artists' models of "Still Life," the great rose window of "Wife-wooing," the patterns on the dead birds in "Pigeon Feathers," and similar elements in most of the other tales show that the architecture of the narrative composition and of the reality it evokes are essentially the same. Updike's artistry and his ontology in this collection strive to approximate and identify each other.

II   *"The Persistence of Desire"*

The second story of *Pigeon Feathers,* "The Persistence of Desire," treats not only the dynamics of vital memory but also a new encounter of the protagonist with the objects of his memory. Clyde Behn, happily married by his own confession and father of two children, returns to Olinger and chances on his lover of many years ago, also married now, in an eye-doctor's office. Their affair had ended painfully, one gathers, and both are upset by the sudden meeting; for they are still attracted to each other and have survived in each other's thoughts. Alone with the girl in the reception room, Clyde asks to meet her again; and later, focusing fuzzily because of the medication in his eyes, he recklessly invades an examining room where she waits alone and pleads before her on his knees. When his treatment is finished, he leaves through the now-crowded waiting room; and, from the blur of figures, the girl arises and puts a note in his shirt pocket, then goes out to her husband who waits in the car. Clyde can't read the note with his distorted pupils, but is made happy and excited by this admission of continued regard.

"The Persistence of Desire" is a curious modern fictive parallel to Wordsworth's famous "Tintern Abbey" poem—that inquiry into the interaction of passion, memory, and the resultant new reality. Like the Wordsworthian narrator, Clyde Behn views himself in a context of strange double identity—his past and present "I"—stimulated by the return to the childhood haunts and especially by the fateful meeting with his old love. He is able to gain a certain objectification of himself against the locale and desire of his past and thus truly to "see himself" briefly for perhaps the first time in his life. The symbolic quality of the action is important. Clyde travels from Massachusetts, his present home, back to Pennsylvania and back into his past. This last is emphasized in Clyde's recognition of how little things have changed. One reason for his return is eye trouble, but the vague and minor difficulty with his sight is as much metaphysical as physical (to call it "psychosomatic" would be just as valid); and Clyde's visit is intended to clarify his vision in both realms. Using a mild irony, Updike has Clyde obtain the greatest precision of inner sight while his eyes are literally blurred by the doctor's drops. In this awkward condition, he achieves a fleeting intimacy with the girl and soon after receives her promise-laden note.

Since Clyde cannot decipher the girl's message, he has not yet gained any decisive knowledge. But the confrontation with the object, or better said "the subject," of his memory makes him suddenly aware of his present spiritual desolation despite his comfortable domestic and vocational situation. When the girls asks him, "aren't you happy?" he replies, "I am, I am; but . . . happiness isn't everything." Clyde learns, simply, "the persistence of desire"—that the price of passion is its permanence and that love relationships, once established, can never be fully undone. For Clyde and Janet such realization may be news both distressing and salutary, for it shows them, however dimly they grasp it, the painful limitations of their human freedom even while it confronts them with the evidence of involuntary human fidelity.

Janet also becomes for Clyde an orienting moment in the flux of life, and the early pages of the story prepare her role. The first sentence mentions the checkerboard pattern of the doctor's office floor, which renews Clyde's childhood feeling of intersection (the basis of an image Updike uses frequently in *Of the Farm*) that now reflects his confused sense of identity, a confusion deriving from the conflicting claims of past and present. When Clyde selects at random a magazine in the waiting room he reads that the cells of the human body completely replace themselves every seven years; and he also contrasts the ultra-modern speedometer clock with the stopped grandfather clock in the same room. In this tension of mutability, then, the old girlfriend (who has changed so little) acts as his hold on time and helps him re-define his precarious identity. One of the duties of love is to provide a stable selfhood through the response of the other; it is not escape but fulfillment. Janet, however temporarily, does that for Clyde; and that is why he, in his alienation, so desperately wants to see her again.

During the examination, Dr. Pennypacker tells Clyde that he has a fungus on his eyelids and prescribes a cure. The mild disease reminds one of the Biblical scales upon the eyes, a stock metaphor for spiritual blindness. In the framework of the story, Janet provides a symbolic diagnosis and healing for Clyde's problem. Her presence first makes him aware of his "scales," his middle-class boredom; but it also offers a projected solution. If he cannot restore the past, he can at least come to knowledgeable, realistic terms with the present. His intuitive utterance that "happiness isn't everything" is, in spite of its cliché format, a troubling insight into truth; for it shows him at last that life is far more complex than he had thought it to be. The message that he cannot read with his unfocused eyes becomes the image for his future: for he *will* be able to see and will then have to choose between the steps to authentic or inauthentic living.

III   *"Pigeon Feathers"*

"Pigeon Feathers," the ninth story in the collection, was included among the O. Henry Prize Short Stories of 1962; and it exemplifies Updike at his best. Its hero, fourteen-year-old David Kern, suffers through a terrifying religious crisis; the force of the tale is in rendering credible the experience of faith and doubt that transpires in an adolescent mind. The story has vague autobiographical contours: David has moved with his family from Olinger to the rural Firetown; and, like the Caldwell family in *The Centaur* and the Robinsons in *Of the Farm*, the Kerns have taken over the ancestral farm at the insistence of the mother and against the wishes of the schoolteacher-father and son. Updike (in the Foreword to *Olinger Stories*) recalls a similar move in his own youth, one from Shillington to Plowtown, that had had a profound effect on his maturation. The ten-mile displacement, he writes, "this strange distance, this less than total remove from my milieu, is for all I know the crucial detachment of my life."[1]

In any case, the resultant double perspective, the sense of existing in two places, precipitates for the hero of the story an alienation that finds expression in a religious dilemma. Already depressed by his new surroundings, David meets the devil in the pages of H. G. Wells' *The Outline of History*; and the boy travels through the doubt and despair that had afflicted the Victorians a century earlier. Wells shatters him with his arguments against the divinity of Jesus; and, soon after, perched in blackness on the outhouse seat at night, David has a horrifying vision of death and of the dizzying infinity of the universe. No one helps him, and months go by while he suffers. One evening, at the instigation of the ancient grandmother, David is asked to kill the pigeons in the barn with the twenty-two caliber rifle he has received for his fifteenth birthday. He shoots six birds the next day while the rest escape; and he then goes to bury the little bodies. In examining the intricate formation of feathers and the colors on the dead pigeons, and in considering their beauty in spite of their worthlessness, he gains assurance that immortality must be in store for him.

The element of displacement is crucial to the story. The move from town to country makes David a self-styled geographical refugee; but, above all, it underscores his condition as a spiritual outsider. But that isolation changes when he learns that all men appear to be outsiders—that religion is an elaborate ruse designed not to help one face death honestly but to cushion its reality. In the town, furthermore, one is sufficiently occupied to avoid a contemplation of death; but, in the country, close to what should be the healing power of nature, one is drawn by the proximity of the soil to darker thoughts of death and decay. The arguments between David's parents about natural and organic farming amplify, for his distressed ears, his anxiety; for the strife about what kills the soil leads him to additional visions of the grave. In his hypertense condition, even the outhouse, resting above the pit of decomposing feces, triggers a horrid nightmare glimpse of a dying universe.

Personal participation in death restores—or first creates—David's faith. The killing of the pigeons is, first of all, a catharsis, a cleansing involvement in violence and destruction that is a microform of the Classical tragic mode. But David, who feels like an avenger in the excitement of the shooting, also attains a measure of understanding about the meaning of death and of divinity in the scheme of being: "He had the sensation of a creator; ... out of each of them he was making a full bird." The analogy, of course, is that man likewise is somehow fulfilled through death and that God in allowing death is not permitting a catastrophic absurdity but a good and necessary consummation. The horror of infinity changes to a trust in its intelligent perfection, unarticulated as its form may be. In the final words of the story, David is "robed in this certainty: that the God who had lavished such craft upon these worthless birds would not destroy His whole creation by refusing to let David live forever."

The culminating action and the conclusion of the story sound suspiciously like a fictional updating of the Scholastic argument from design for God's existence, and one should not be inattentive to the possible irony in the whole performance. After all, the line of logic from a half-dozen dead pigeons to a boy's new assurance of personal immortality is broken by numerous forensic short circuits. But that philosophical argument is not the point of the story, nor should it be the center of criticism regarding the story. The point is that Updike, through symbolic action and analogy, has written a moving religious narrative that does not presume to convince one of the objective truth of Christian faith but that does testify to an individual's achievement of it.

"Pigeon Feathers" employs a design and designs to attest to the fact of, or at least the faith in, cosmic design. Beyond that, the action represents an archetypal maturation ritual, a personal coming-of-age of a young man who is not satisfied by the formal ecclesiastical rites (catechism and confirmation) but who uses worldly implements (above all the gun) to fight through the trauma toward adulthood. Beyond this ritual, the narrative is a concentrated history of modern man's struggle to assert himself in a lonely universe. The bleak generalities of an H. G. Wells, the neuroses of despairing late Victorians, the conspiracy of silence among twentieth-century Christians forced to compromise their dogmas—all these stagger the innocent generation and demand that it fashion its own unique bondage or freedom. The answers that its representatives find, those who are healthy enough, are molded from the stuff of daily trivia. If the path from six dead pigeons to a God who cares seems absurd, it is no more so than the tortuous directions mapped by wise men of the past few centuries.

IV *"You'll Never Know, Dear, How Much I Love You"*

The twelfth story, "You'll Never Know, Dear, How Much I Love You," is superficially like Joyce's famous "Araby" in the *Dubliners* collection. Updike's boy also hurries to a carnival; poor, charged with excitement and anticipation, full of the adolescent's romantic yearnings, he is eager to offer himself to the mysterious and glittering world; and he is disappointed by the world's rejection. Admittedly, a lesser story than "Araby" because it lacks the symbolic density of that tale, Updike's story succeeds, nonetheless, on its own terms.

Ben is a ten-year-old Olinger child (the town is not named, but Updike includes the narrative in his *Olinger Stories*) who receives fifty cents from his parents to visit the traveling carnival that has just arrived in town that day. He races to the site at dusk, moves from booth to booth trying to absorb everything, buys a cotton candy, and then places all the remaining coins, one by one, on the board where the numbers wheel is whirling. He loses everything, his last forty cents, and turns to go; but the attendant calls him back and, with rough insulting kindness, returns thirty cents to him and tells him to leave. Ben departs embarrassed and disgraced, feeling cheated by this encounter with a misunderstanding adult world.

The fragile story depends upon the inversion of a metaphor for its effect. The world is represented as a gaudy woman, but here she does not seduce the innocent. Young Ben goes out gladly to be taken, to be embraced by her, but she will not have him; and he is thrust back into his childishness. The stock vehicles of temptation are present (sex, gambling), but Ben is too young to be corrupted; he can only be thrust out of the way as an annoyance when he merely wants the exhilaration of participation. He does not care that he has lost his nickels to the numbers wheel; to be able to play at all is enough for him. What is ultimately humiliating to him is that he is given the doubtful favor of the returned coins and thus singled out as unworthy of the world.

The title is part of the refrain from "You Are My Sunshine," the sadly sweet pop tune that every generation revives in its own beat. The girls dressed in white cowboy garb—cheap Americana —sing it at the carnival; and, filtered through Ben's tumescent young consciousness, it comes to represent both his naïve longing for an illusive, falsely bright world and the transparent quality of the beckoning entertainment realm.

The story is not profound, and it will not do to take it too seriously. Updike himself connects it with "The Persistence of Desire" by noting that the "optically bothered Clyde Behn seems to me a late refraction of that child Ben who flees the carnival with 'tinted globes confusing his eyelashes.'" But Ben, as Updike also says, is "a pure Olinger child" who even in his unhappy adventure is being protected by the world .from the world itself.[2] The alienation he feels is the result, paradoxically, of compassion and not the lack of it. Ben still roams inside Eden.

V "A & P"

The fourteenth story of *Pigeon Feathers*, entitled "A & P," is one of Updike's most popular; and it has been anthologized in college and commercial collections. It is indeed one of the brilliant pieces that redeem the few pages of inferior writing in the book. Sammy, the narrator, is a nineteen-year-old working as a checkout clerk in the A & P market on a Thursday afternoon. The scene is an unnamed Massachusetts town (Tarbox of *Couples*?) north of Boston and "five miles from a beach, with a big summer colony out on the Point."

Into the staid store in this staid place walk three girls barefoot and in swimming suits, probably the daughters of wealthy summer residents from the Point. The store is not accustomed to such casualness, and the girls cause a small sensation while they shop. They buy only a jar of herring snacks and are about to pay at Sammy's checkout when Lengel, the store manager and a dour man who "teaches Sunday School and the rest," sees them. He comes forward to chide them for what to him is their indecency. The girls are flustered, but they stand up to him, especially the cool, regal one in a tempting suit who, Sammy guesses, is used to snobbier markets than this one. Sammy quickly rings up the bill and gives the girls their purchase. As they leave, he tells Lengel, "I quit"; punctuates the manager's surprised protests by banging up a "No Sale" on the register; and walks out. Outside, the bathing-suit trio has already gone; and Sammy is left with a sharp, painful revelation of "how hard the world was going to be to me hereafter."

Updike has Sammy narrate the story in a breezy, late-teenage vernacular; the brashness and occasional mild vulgarity of the language balance nicely the inherent sentimentality of the action. Sammy's references to one girl's breasts as "the two smoothest scoops of vanilla I had ever known" and to another girl as passable "raw material" cut the saccharine flavor of his impulsive and romantic gesture. Updike also alternates between the past and historical present tenses to provide a tight little dramatic episode that his fiction does not often exhibit. Since the tale builds upon an increasing tension of embarrassment, the play-by-play technique of the present tense description heightens the precise moments of strain and offers the reader, at the same time, a vicarious participation.

"A & P" is also one of the very few Updike stories (before the Henry Bech tales), that ventures into comedy, and this comedic quality is achieved through the tempered humor of the clever phrase and through the incongruous action that is meant to hold the slight pathos within its prescribed limits. In the end, as one might expect, the humor evolves an ironic element; for the smart remarks of the supermarket employees and the indignant stares of the customers do not really subject the girls to ridicule but expose instead the provinciality of their audience. The girls have class; the town does not; but Sammy, caught somewhere in the middle, makes the story. With a single act he achieves a new integrity, one that divorces him from his unthinking conservative environment and leaves him, not with a suddenly developed affinity to the wealthy set, but with a loneliness that signals his birth into alienation.

Sammy's reaction is the reflex of the still uncorrupted, of the youth still capable of the grand gesture because he has not learned the sad wisdom of compromise. But therein lie the pathos and the refreshing rashness of the story. Sammy's reckless vitality is echoed by the fancied percussion of the cash register: "Hello (*bing*) there, you (*gung*) hap-py *pee*-pul (*splat*)!" The undertone of sorrow resides in the depressing sight that awaits Sammy outside the supermarket: the girls for whom he has gallantly sacrificed his job have disappeared; in their place is a young married woman yelling at her spoiled children, a much commoner refrain to the heady tunes of wish-

ful American romance. Bare beauty could brighten even the
A & P; but since it is dangerously out of place there, it must
be exorcised to safeguard the sorry successes of Grundyism.

VI *"Lifeguard"*

The speaker in this story is a youthful divinity student
who spends his summers on an unnamed New England beach
as a lifeguard. He self-consciously uses the props and duties of
his summer vocation as a tangible metaphor of his future pas-
toral profession. The tower on which he perches is the pulpit;
the Red Cross emblem on the back of his chair, the Christian
symbol; the bathers and sunners his congregation (it *is* a Sunday
morning); and he himself, the alert guardian of souls. His
sermon-monologue turns on the unity of spirit and body, and
he considers himself to be a person in whom the two are perfectly married. In reality he is quite puritanic, overly aware of
the flesh, and attempts in a manner more Sophist than Protestant to justify his lust. "Every seduction is a conversion" emerges
as the message of his discourse, but he is far more absorbed in
a loving quasi-sublimation of his sexuality than in any serious
hermeneutic; and, like the speakers in Browning's dramatic
monologues, he reveals more of his own hidden psyche than
of observed and interpreted truth.

"Lifeguard" is a homily, although its novice preacher is
musing to an imagined audience; and it has the traditional sermon format: an introduction, a statement of the text, exposition,
bountiful illustrations, and concluding exhortation. But it is also
a sermon parody and, withal, a confession—an exposé by one
formally inside yet privately outside the edifice of theological
endeavor. The irony of the story is that, despite the young
student's insight, he does not see at all. He is surrounded by
people to whom he is supposedly learning to minister, but he
has no relationship with humanity. He is caught in an immense
egotism that feeds on theology when theology ought instead to
show him the way of humility. He is as isolated and alienated,
in a profession dedicated to joining and reconciling humanity,
as the other characters in this collection.

Here again Updike has employed design to explicate design.
The formal sermon structure is a vehicle, in this instance, that
destroys the very substance of its text. The student preaches on

the affinity of spirit and flesh; but his discourse is, in more ways than one, all flesh. It is a model of design, but it has no vitality. In a final irony, the young man disproves, by what he is, the very contention that he so skillfully argues. Spirit and flesh may very well be more intimately related than Pauline and Augustinian dualism have comprehended them to be; but, if they are, the way toward realizing that unity is through a passionate involvement—not a logical exercise—that the young man can elaborate upon but has never experienced. Even his own acute sense of irony cannot redeem him; for, purely intellectual, it lacks existential dimension.

VII   *The Jack and Clare Stories*

Of the fourteen other stories in *Pigeon Feathers*, three are casually connected through the appearance of the same family. A young couple, Jack and Clare, living somewhere in the vicinity of Boston, are the personae in "Walter Briggs," "Should Wizard Hit Mommy?" and "The Crow in the Woods." In "Walter Briggs," Jack and family are returning home at night from Boston. To pass the time, husband and wife reminisce about their first months of married life together as employees at a Y.M.C.A. camp (Updike and his wife did something of the same thing shortly after their marriage). In recalling the names of persons at the camp, they encounter the image of a fat bridge player whose last name eludes them. At home later and in bed beside his sleeping wife, Jack sifts through the camp memories again and finds the name. "Walter Briggs," he tells Clare, "knowing he wouldn't wake her."

The technical trick of the story is in constructing narration on the basis of a frustrating phenomenon that everyone has experienced—the memory block that eventually yields to probing and gives one some old bit of knowledge that the efforts at recall have magnified far out of proportion. In this story too the recovery of the name is not the important thing in itself; rather, the name is the cryptic key that opens the shared life of the past. And that, in turn, is significant not because the events were anything but commonplace but because they were shared. Irrelevant things assume meaning through the numinous energy of affection; and, in the extremely private code of this marital dialogue, to say "Walter Briggs" is to rediscover a forgotten pleasure of one's life—like finding an heirloom one had some-how misplaced. That Jack speaks to his slumbering wife makes no difference; he is simply affirming his joy about and satisfaction from their mutual past.

"Should Wizard Hit Mommy?" finds the same couple in less concord. A Freudian tale quite like "Incest" in *The Same Door* collection, in it the attraction between father and small daughter develops a subtle animosity between husband and wife, daughter and mother. Jack tells his daughter, now almost four, a spontaneous story about skunks in a futile attempt to make her take a Saturday afternoon nap. When he climaxes his narration with a dramatic description of Mommy Skunk's striking a cruel magician, the little girl is upset and insists on a retaliatory sequel: the wizard should hit Mommy back.

Updike uses the old frame story technique—the tale within a tale—in an atmosphere of innocence to produce a mild shock for the reader. Instead of the cozy association that the bed-time story usually prompts, a shadow of elemental violence and hatred darkens the scene, one made all the more unnerving since it is cast by a small child. Little Jo identifies Mommy Skunk with her own mother and demands punishment for her violation of a taboo—defying the preternatural. Her perverse behavior is obviously born out of fantasy and the unconscious, and therefore it is excusable but is, nonetheless, frightening. The daughter instinctively wishes the rival-mother dead, and the father succumbs as well by siding with the child against his wife—who is pregnant and therefore carrying a potential threat to his dominant maleness. Whether or not one accepts such transparent Freudian interpretation, the story succeeds in conveying the aura of primitive fear that invades the common-place of a modern civilized household.

In "The Crow in the Woods," Jack arises on an early winter morning to tend to his baby daughter (the couple's only child in this story). Still blurry from an alcoholic party the night be-fore and from lovemaking later, he nevertheless sees things with the hyperclarity of overwrought senses. His wife joins them and makes breakfast; with the food before him, Jack sees a nature epiphany through the window: a huge black bird lands in the snow-covered woods close by and sends flakes drifting down in beautiful confusion. He calls to his wife in an instant of joy, but she answers only, "Eat your egg." Cold

sobriety destroys the ecstatic moment; the lovemaking communion of the night before dissolves in the practical necessities of
daily living.

In these stories one finds a progression of marital states
although the chronology of the family development is not consistent. The movement is a retreat and a construction of individual defenses by the marriage partners. In this most vulnerable of relationships, the initial amity of "Walter Briggs" changes
to the guilty hostility of "Wizard" and crystallizes into the
cautious pragmatism of "The Crow in the Woods." In the last
story, Jack is ignored by his wife as he reveals his bared
soul. That is the climax and conclusion of the narrative, but
the projected implication is clear: even the most intimate
conditions offer no guarantee against alienation. Estrangement
can become a reflex of normalcy, and that is what makes the
possibility especially frightening.

VIII   *Other Marriage Tales*

Five other stories in *Pigeon Feathers* occur in the marriage
arena. "Dear Alexandros," the least successful of them or of
all the tales in the book, is too obviously a gimmick narrative—
too contrived, it is yet too diffuse in its focus. The story consists of two letters: one from a poor child in Greece to his
"adoptive" parents in Connecticut who partially support him
with monthly checks; the other an answer from the "father," a
Mr. Kenneth Bentley now residing in New York. One learns
from the American reply that the couple have separated; a tone
of embarrassment and apology echoes through Bentley's letter.
The story is at least a noble failure, for it founders by trying
to do too much. The gimmick is in the language: Alexandros'
letter is a translation, while Bentley's is composed with an eye
toward *its* translation into Greek; and the formality of diction
and phrase in both contrasts with the effort at genuine, needful
communication.

The ironic revelation that appears through the epistolary
exchange is that the wealthy Americans, who would be charitable
toward poor foreigners, cannot keep their own house in order.
They suffer a poverty of spirit, a disease of bountiful living,
that is worse than the Greek boy's physical deprivation. But
Updike packs a surfeit of social commentary into this brief story.

The references to United States-Russian political relations, to the Greek Classics, and to American drinking habits only pad the slight narrative until it is nearly stifled by its trimmings.

"Wife-wooing" employs the rare second-person singular perspective; for the speaker addresses his wife throughout the narration in the "you" form. Plot is almost wholly lacking; instead, one finds descriptions of casually transpiring domestic action that carry archetypal and symbolic significance. A young couple sitting before their fireplace with their two small children, eating hamburgers and french fries purchased from a nearby drive-in, become the post-types of primitive humans who hunted and killed their sustenance and devoured it around the fire in the cave dwelling. Out of this parallel the speaker fashions the avatar of the elemental woman whom his wife represents. Whether she is in prehistory or sitting bare-thighed before a suburban hearth, she is fertility, domesticity, security. In the woman the man has his fulfillment, and to "woo" her is to court the elusive components of his own identity.

The Medieval image of the rose window, symbol of both purity and defloration, supports the religious nature of the man's total commitment to the marriage event. Through intercourse, through the rose window, the male sees into the design of himself and his world in a new sense. This Gothic pattern helps define also the male relationship to contemporary woman and clarifies the conclusion of the story. The wife, like the elemental woman and the Holy Virgin, has an earnest of grace for the man that he depends upon but that he may not take for granted. When, at the end, the wife comes to her husband in bed eager for sexual love, it is a gift that he must recognize and accept as such: it is as old as human history yet as new and unique as the individuality of experiencing can make it.

"Home" is a delightful and moving account of a young Pennsylvanian's return to his native area after a year in England. Robert (a mathematics teacher), his wife Joanne, and baby Corinne travel from the New York port, where their liner has docked, to the Pennsylvania small town with Robert's parents. The story, again essentially plotless, is structured by the movement westward of car and passengers toward the old parental home. The land and the people seem alien to Robert and Joanne; they are undergoing culture shock. But the tension dissolves through an incident that Robert's irrepressibly curious schoolteacher-father precipitates. On the final stretch toward home, the father overtakes and startles a fat Pennsylvania Dutchman who is incautiously driving a large new car. When the Dutchman catches up to them, enraged and swearing, Robert's father stops his car; the Dutchman does likewise and walks back for an altercation. In the funny scene involving the Dutchman's redfaced obscenity and the father's dogged curiosity, Robert joins the argument in his own native Dutch accent (expertly reproduced by the author); and, through the unpleasantries, he finds a re-entry, for his wife as well as himself, into the familiar past.

"The Astronomer" has as its protagonist the young man Walter who, in a condition of cosmic anxiety or of ontological *angst,* reads Kierkegaard as an antidote. He and his wife are visited in their Riverside Drive apartment by a Hungarian astronomer, an old friend from college days. The narrator fears the conversation, for the brilliant astronomer's cold acceptance of the Einsteinian universe and his familiarity with a mathematically plumbed infinity threaten the precarious scaffoldry of religious faith that Walter has erected. But later in the evening the guest confesses to a moment of terror in his life when he had been frightened by the American landscape while traveling through a barren stretch of New Mexico. That revelation heartens the young host: his friend also knows fear, is vulnerable and fallible; and, therefore, Walter's edifice of belief can logically stand.

Two deft tricks enhance this story. One is ironic reversal: Walter's terror springs from the mysteries of the heavens, but his friend who knows the secrets of space confesses to the fear of an earthly commonplace. The second device is a double unifying metaphor at the end of the story: after the astronomer's admission of fear, Walter sees the mess of coffee dregs, ashes, and wine glasses as a parallel to the "universal debris" that in his mind clutters outer space. His living room provides a microcosm of the universe that is comforting because it is familiar. But then this apartment hanging in darkness above the Hudson River seems to him a single inhabited star, and he is back again in the mild suffering of cosmic loneliness. Once more Updike employs the theme of natural design with his own esthetic patterns to stress human isolation.

The last of these marriage tales, "The Doctor's Wife," has for

its setting a remote island in the Bahamas. Ralph and Eve, a
young American couple, are vacationing there; and, in the
particular incident that comprises the narrative, they submit
to a malicious grilling by an English physician's bigoted wife
regarding the possibility of Negro blood in Eve because of her
dark tan. When Eve leaves to tend her children, Ralph is left
alone with the Englishwoman. He overdefends his wife and
thereby betrays her, for she is fiercely liberal and would just
as soon be identified with a black heritage as not. Whether Eve
is in fact partly Negro is left unclear (although she probably
is not), but it obviously doesn't matter. The point is that the
poison of prejudice can infect even an established marriage
and compromise the integrity of the partners.

The predatory quality of the story is imaged mainly by the
shark motif. The Englishwoman with her pointed face is shark-
like, just as her conversation circles hungrily around the information she desires. But Ralph, corrupted by the woman's calculated hatred, also feels the lust to destroy. When he flees into
the sea and hangs there, fearing the literal sharks and the
cruel woman on land, he is enduring the punishment and the
absolution for his cowardice. Malevolent design in nature
informs the evil impulses in men's hearts.

IX   *Late Adolescence in Olinger*

Two other Olinger tales in this collection could well be preliminary sketches for *The Centaur*. In "Flight," which concerns
a love-hate relationship between an introspective teenage boy
(an only child) and his histrionic mother, the title connotes the
painful ambivalence of the boy's position. His life seems poised
for "flight" in the sense of a brilliant career awaiting him, and
his mother uses the metaphor of flying to encourage him. But
the disappointment of her own failed vocational dreams causes
her to place a pressure on her son that is often quite intolerable;
as a result, the possibility of flight means also an escape from
her neurotic presence. The double use of the term could be
modeled after Joyce's bird imagery in *A Portrait of the Artist
as a Young·Man*; and, like Stephen Dedalus, Updike's Allen Dow
turns to sexuality for inspiration and relief. He acquires a girl
friend while on a trip with the school debating team; Molly
Bingaman, pretty but dull (like Penny in *The Centaur*), becomes

a weapon for Allen to wield against his mother and also a source
of security against his late-adolescent estrangement from himself.

Molly is ultimately unattainable for Allen; her earthiness
and her higher social status in Olinger put her out of reach. She
is part of the normal small-town milieu that Updike's semi-
autobiographical heroes can never quite inhabit—something like
Thomas Mann's tormented esthetes—and Updike himself, in the
Foreword to *Olinger Stories,* remarks that Molly represents
enchantment of distance that plagues his sensitive young men.
Allen gives up Molly at last to please his mother, but the price
she pays is her son's liberation from her domination. He tells
her, at least, that this battle is the last between them that she
will win.

In "A Sense of Shelter," the counterpart story to "Flight,"
young William, the bright, stuttering Olinger High School senior, confesses love to his classmate, the beautiful Mary Landis.
William is an outsider; his relation to Mary is like a later version
of Charlie's infatuation with Gloria in "The Alligators." Mary herself is an evolution (or degeneration) of Gloria, the classroom
queen who blossoms too fast in the hothouse of adulation and
starts to fade even before she finishes high school. Mary is still
lovely but jaded and bored, a girl excited too young by sex and
otherwise condemned to provinciality. Since Mary and William
have known each other since childhood, the pathos of the story
comes through the social and emotional distance that grows between them, even though they remain casually intimate. Mary has
the greater, accelerated maturity; but William has the promising
professional future ahead of him, and his impulsive proposal of
marriage to her is both a gesture to the community and an
attempt to take along something of his adolescence into adulthood. Mary refuses him, of course, and William is relieved. He
has paid a ritual obeisance to the small-town code (to sow his
wild oats and then settle down in an early local marriage) and
been given his freedom. Now he can pursue, in his methodical
way, the sober dream of an academic career.

But the melancholy fact is that William is not really free:
he is only trading the "sense of shelter" that the Olinger schools
and classmates have provided him for a thoroughly planned,
totally orthodox and secure professional career. The "Lavender
Blue" lyrics that he croons to himself add an ironic gloss. He is
not "king" nor is Mary his "queen"; they are both slaves of con-

vention—and such is the gap between the American romantic vision and American reality.

X *New and Old Places, Fragments and Catch-Alls*

"Still Life," the third story in *Pigeon Feathers*, stands by itself because of its unique setting. Leonard Hartz is a talented young American studying art under the "GI Bill" at the Constable School in England. He is attracted to an eighteen-year-old British student at the school, Robin Cox, who substitutes vivaciousness for artistic ability. "Still Life" aptly describes the nature of their relationship, for they never become more than cautious friends. Leonard is moved to jealousy at one point when an American acquaintance asks Robin to pose in the nude for him (she refuses), but even his jealousy leads nowhere. Their friendship seems metaphoric of stock British-American affinities: congenial but confused, sharing some common cultural traditions that invite familiarity but also disguise the essential differences not so easily overcome. Again, the presence of self-conscious literal design in the art-school setting reinforces the concern for patterns of existence that marks this collection.

"Archangel" is a cryptic page-and-a-half sketch that at best illustrates Updike's curious interest in blending archaic and modern imagery. The "archangel" is obviously the narrator, but his identity beyond that is hard to fathom. He is, variously, a suitor celebrating the pleasures of luxurious love in the idiom of the Renaissance courtiers, the muse addressing the author (a clever reversal of the usual invocation), and perhaps the author talking to a reluctant audience. But, apart from the rich texture of language, the story offers little. It is not poetry, in spite of its lush imagery, nor is it narrative fiction; and since Updike has not chosen to develop it in any other direction, one is not obliged to take it seriously.

The next to the last story of the collection could have been more fortunately located in the "First Person Singular" section of *Assorted Prose*. Encumbered by the unwieldy title of "The Blessed Man of Boston, My Grandmother's Thimble, and Fanning Island," the story, one guesses, has only the thinnest veneer of invention over autobiography; indeed, it seems to serve as a catch-all for the reminiscences that Updike has not completely refined into fiction. The family memories and personal recollections are beautifully recorded; but, because the author has not provided the universality of true fiction, the artistic relevance is limited.

The final story, in contrast, is of the same nature as "The Blessed Man...," but it succeeds precisely where that one fails. It has a similar exhaustive title—"Packed Dirt, Church-going, A Dying Cat, A Traded Car"—but a much greater internal unity and continuity. Above all, it does transform personal memory into something universally meaningful. If "The Blessed Man..." is a catch-all for the stories Updike would have liked to write and did not, "Packed Dirt..." draws together many of those he did create into a new composition and a new vision.

David Kern, the protagonist of "Pigeon Feathers," is the narrator of this story. He is now a mature family man, father of four children, living in the neighborhood of Boston in the locale of the "A & P" tale. (In the course of this essay-story Updike returns also to Olinger, Alton, Greenwich Village, Manhattan's Upper West Side, Oxford, and the Caribbean Islands, collecting old motifs and images along the way.) Now a writer, David Kern still suffers from the cosmic vertigo that had frightened him as a fourteen-year-old boy. Diverted by lust, or driving to see his father hospitalized by a heart attack, or attending a cat struck by an automobile—his participation in the major and minor accidents of life reminds him both of the preciousness and brevity of his moment in time and space.

Young David in "Pigeon Feathers" finds solace and hope for immortality in a classic theological manner, by extending the evidence of design in nature to the universal design of divinity. The adult David no longer expresses his fears or faith so naïvely, but his approach to being and his defense against nihilism remain essentially the same. When he declares at the end of "Packed Dirt..." that "we in America need ceremonies," he is suggesting that the various rituals for approaches and depar-tures, for being and death, impose at least a provisional order—an order that substitutes for the religiously based traditional order that is fading fast.

XI *The Reconstructive Ritual*

When the unexpected gift that characterizes *The Same Door* stories is no longer forthcoming to people, as is often the case in

Pigeon Feathers, alienation is the result. It is alienation in many forms: isolation from the community, estrangement from those who used to be closest to one, and loneliness in the midst of the universe itself. But Updike's people seldom remain aimlessly drifting in a spiritual vagrancy; for such drifting is a luxury that the residual work ethic, embodied in Updike's own artistic persistence, will not allow. His characters continue to go through the motions, and the repetition of the daily actions settles into new rituals that can generate, perhaps, new meaning. It is not that the unexpected gift no longer occasionally arrives; rather, it will not do for people to languish in hope for it. Grace still responds to the stimulus of works, and one must fashion his own design to recover the outlines of a master pattern.

CHAPTER 5

The Centaur:
Guilt through Redemption

> Let us not mock God with metaphor,
> analogy, sidestepping, transcendence;
> making of the event a parable, a sign painted
>   in the faded credulity of earlier ages:
> let us walk through the door.
>   —from "Seven Stanzas at Easter"

I Myth and Story

THE CENTAUR, published in 1963, is the most ambitious of Updike's works before *Couples*; and it is also the one that has been most extravagantly praised and most vehemently damned. Longer and more intricate than *Rabbit, Run*, this novel became a best seller and also won the National Book Award for Fiction in 1964. While some reviewers greeted the book as the first evidence of Updike's willingness to confront the so-called larger-than-life issues, others called it a *roman manqué* at best and a "sell-out" to the popular fashions of fiction at worst. The aspect of the novel that bothered most critics was Updike's blend—or forced combination—of Classical myth and realistic narrative. Even a sympathetic commentator such as Arthur Mizener considered the Chiron-Prometheus material an unwise and artistically unrealized addition to the contemporary Olinger fiction.[1]

The novel begins with the attempt of George Caldwell, a middle-aged science teacher at Olinger High School, to interest an unruly class in evolutionary human history. Caldwell is also Chiron the centaur, part man and part stallion, and the mentor of the young Greek heroes. Caldwell is wounded in the ankle by a missile thrown by one of his students (the parallel mythic

80

action is Chiron struck by a stray poisoned arrow shot by a battling centaur); he limps next door to Hummel's garage (Hephaestus' forge) to have the missile removed. Returning as Chiron, he surprises Venus bathing in her forest pool (Vera Hummel the physical education teacher emerging from a locker-room shower) and, warned by the thunder of Zeus, resists her seductive advances. Back in the classroom, he strikes the obstreperous pupil Deifendorf (Hercules) with the arrow while Zimmerman the principal (Zeus) watches.

In the second chapter, the thirtyish Peter Caldwell recounts the experiences of the few winter days of early 1947, fourteen years earlier, that led to the "death" of George Caldwell, his teacher-father. Peter, now a "second-rate abstract expressionist" painter living in a Manhattan loft, narrates to his sleeping Negro mistress the initial events of those days: arising on a cold Monday morning to prepare for school, listening to the family conversation about his father's hypochondria, rushing late to school with his father, and picking up an obscene hitchhiker on the way. Following the brief interlude of Chapter Three (Chiron and his Olympian students), Peter resumes his reminiscence in Chapter Four. On that same Monday afternoon in the past, George Caldwell has been X-rayed for suspected stomach cancer; in the evening, the father and son plan to return home from a swimming meet in the nearby Alton Y.M.C.A., but, when the old family Buick does not start, they stay overnight in a cheap Alton hotel and walk to school in Olinger the next morning.

Chapter Five presents, abruptly and without any explanation, George Caldwell's obituary, which is written in the style of a small-town newspaper by one of Caldwell's former pupils. Chapter Six, a Surrealistic dream sequence, has Peter as Prometheus grieving over his father's death; but then he meets his father (still in the dream) and pleads with him to go on living. Chapter Seven, which shifts to a third-person narration, depicts George Caldwell's conversation and actions with his fellow faculty members and Peter's fumbling pettings with Penny, his teenage girlfriend, at the evening basketball game. That night on the way home, the Buick stalls in a snowbank; and father and son are again marooned. Chapter Eight resumes Peter's own narration. He and his father have stayed overnight at the Hummels. By morning the area is snowed in and the schools are closed. In late afternoon, when the Buick is ready to go once more, the two Caldwells drive home, only to stall again on the long, snow-clogged dirt road that leads to their farm. They walk to the house. George tells his wife that the X-rays show him to be free of the feared cancer. Peter becomes sick from the exertion of the past days and stays in bed the next morning (Saturday) with a fever while his father leaves the house, one guesses to dig out the car. In Chapter Nine, Caldwell, now as Chiron, walks out to the black Buick, which he recognizes as the chariot of Zeus, and yields to death.

II   Surrealist and Cubist Analogues

An evaluation of the myth-realism blend depends on a right understanding of how it works. Updike is not writing allegory, for both dimensions of narrative in The Centaur are literally present: the modern fictive creation and the ancient legend that it approximates; thus there is nothing to allegorize. Nor is he simply composing, as Mizener has already correctly observed, updated versions of the Classical myths à la the method of John Erskine a few decades ago. His method and achievement can best be appreciated through analogies to Surrealist and Cubist painting. The intention and the effect of the double narrative in The Centaur are to expand literal reality through distortion—as in Surrealism (with its accompanying psychological expressive modes)—and through the simultaneous projection of many facets of a personality or action, as in Cubism. Since fiction, like all language, is temporally and spatially linear, one cannot, obviously, create the meaningful distortion and dislocation of reality and the simultaneous "thereness" of its aspects as the visual and plastic arts can. One uses, instead, the material of fiction to convert its necessary linearity into the illusion of what one would call, in literary terms, supra-Realism or multi-Realism.

Literary analogies to Surrealism appear, for example, at the beginning and end of Chapter One, in the scene at Hummel's garage and then in the last few minutes of Caldwell's science-class lecture; in the dream sequence of Chapter Six; and in the concluding chapter in the description of Chiron's death. In all of these scenes the absence of a logical sequentiality, of cause and effect, renders the Surrealist impression. In the early scene of the first chapter, Hummel's garage (also Hephaestus' smithy)

gains a Surrealist quality through the constant movement between myth and realistic narrative. The lame blacksmith uses an
acetylene torch and a wire cutter to remove the arrow from Caldwell's ankle, and he is helped by a one-eyed boy who is also a
Cyclops. The scene is precisely detailed yet impossible to believe
—blacksmiths and garage mechanics are not surgeons—until one
realizes that the equine Chiron would indeed be tended by a
smith, and that the action literally concerns Caldwell's car, which
has an important part in the story otherwise. Helped by later
comments in the novel, one can reconstruct the Surrealist scene:
George Caldwell, struck in the ankle by a strange missile in the
classroom, is Chiron the centaur wounded by a poisoned arrow;
but Chiron's body also merges with Caldwell's car, and the
operation in the garage is not the removal of a literal arrow—
George retires to the garage to recover from a merely verbal
shaft—but the repair of the Buick grille that Deifendorf, the
obstreperous pupil, broke. The mingling of animal and mechanical qualities is a characteristic Surrealist device used effectively
here mainly to destroy conventional concepts of time. To be
forced to identify the ancient legendary centaur with a modern
automobile shocks the intellect and imagination into an acceptance of atemporality that Updike needs for the success of his
story.

Surrealism developed from the voguish fascination with psychoanalysis in the first third of the twentieth century, and it is
fitting, therefore, that the Freudian-tinted dream passage com-
prising Chapter Six should borrow the Surrealist style. The
chapter begins with the teenaged Peter in a posture of suffering: "As I lay on my rock various persons visited me." The
reference is obviously mythological—Prometheus chained to his
mountain—but it assumes many other valid meanings. Following Chapter Five as it does (the obituary chapter), it seems
to reveal Peter transfixed in grief over the death of his father.
The town personae who emerge and fade, at any rate, are
like the mourners at a funeral who come to offer condolences to
the immediate bereaved.

But Peter lying on his rock can also be the boy in suspense,
waiting to learn the fateful results of his father's X-ray tests.
Or again, Peter's torture can be his awakening sexuality. His
embarrassment over his biological changes, his misunderstood
mixture of lust and ·curiosity figure in the anguish (insignifi-

cant to the adult but real to the awkward adolescent) represented by the Promethean punishment, particularly since the
archetypal creativity of Prometheus, usually understood in its
artistic aspects, can have sexual, progenitive connotations as
well. And, finally, the torture of Prometheus has a literal parallel
in the incessant itching of Peter's psoriasis—a modern, decidedly
unromantic but nonetheless maddening variation of the legendary eagle that tears daily at Prometheus' liver.

One cannot classify these many uses of the myth as a complex
symbolic device (instead of insisting on the Surrealist analogy)
because they do not function in traditional literary-symbolic
terms. All of these "meanings" of the Prometheus-Peter combination are manifestly present through the distortion that the
dream context creates and are not the result of subtly placed
hints that the reader must decode. As in non-literal painting,
one must grasp the *Gestalt* of the total scene in its equally
significant multi-meanings and interrelations instead of trying
to discover a cryptic key that logically explains the story. This
absence of some dominant literal meaning in favor of the configurational construct provides the particularly powerful expression of reality that conventional symbolism cannot produce.
One sacrifices a coherent story line for the impact of a total
imaginative-emotional approach, but is a worthwhile trade.

One recognizes the quality of Updike's artistic risk in the
final chapter, for in it he depends utterly upon the Surrealist
method to carry the culminating sense of the story. Instead of
presenting Caldwell's death in straightforward fashion and pro-
voking a symbolic interpretation, Updike inverts the process. He
shows only Chiron the centaur in the final scene and surrounds the
circumstances of his death with a mythic opacity: "Chiron
accepted death." Does that imply that Caldwell, his modern
parallel, also dies? It is possible, as one reviewer maintained,
that Chiron's death is symbolic of Caldwell's existential resig-
nation—that he does not die physically, in love with death as
he is, but chooses, for the sake of family and vocational duty,
to return to the hell of daily teaching. The strategy of the Surrealist technique here is to give concluding emphasis to the
combination of compassion and irony that pervades the novel.
The compassion is bound up both in the myth and in the modern
narrative. Chiron dies so that Prometheus may be expiated and
liberated; Caldwell decides to go on living to serve his pro-

fession as teacher and fulfill his responsibility as family man, even
though he is obsessed with death.

Although it is a bit confusing to speak of a myth behind
the myth, an overriding archetypal pattern does determine the
moral and social substance of *The Centaur,* just as it does in
Updike's other novels. Whereas *The Poorhouse Fair* displayed
the godless City of God and *Rabbit, Run* the quest for a nonexistent Grail, *The Centaur* projects the paradoxical action of
a redemption *into* guilt. This strange redemption utilizes the
other analogy from the visual arts, the Cubist style. Wylie Sypher,
who has examined the relationship of Cubism to fiction, says
that the Cubist influence asserts itself in the twentieth century
in the use of simultaneous perspective, in the strategy of "situating" the story between fact and fiction, in the dependence upon
camouflage and counterfeit, and in the collage technique.[2]
Without subscribing to a belief in Cubist attitudes and goals
(it is, after all, no longer a vital style), Updike does work with
these elements to a degree in his third novel. In *The Centaur,*
the first and fourth Cubist influences, as Sypher describes them,
are most obvious. The configurational structure of multi-meanings
in the myth-realism blend, approached from the intrinsic and
subjective view of Surrealism, becomes from the Cubist focus
a *Gestalt* of simultaneous perspectives. Thus, when one asks
what the formal point of view of *The Centaur* is, one discovers
that it has none. It is mainly Peter's story; but Peter is, at the
same time, a teenager and an adult; he reminisces lucidly but
also recollects from the subconscious; he speaks in the first-
person singular confessional and also with his father inhabits a
scenic point of view—one done, moreover, in the historical present tense that makes those days in 1947 seem dramatically immediate. Even those chapters that exclude Peter as character have
the sense of his presence, as if they were to be understood from
the position of Peter the mature artist who is refashioning his
father's past and thereby his own. In these ways, then, the simultaneous perspective of the Cubist style informs *The Centaur.*

Updike uses the collage technique even more obviously. The
nine chapters of the novel with their various forms of narrative
—myth-realism, confession, idyll, obituary, confession, dream,
broad scene, confession, myth—compose a collage, while the
seventh chapter (the broad scene) forms a smaller representative collage of its own. More difficult to describe, but signifi-

cantly present, are the Cubist "situating" of narrative and the
use of camouflage. Updike does not depend as necessarily as
André Gide (whom Sypher discusses), for example, on transformed reportage or on history as the basis of his fiction, nor
does he capitalize on the tensions between plot and autobiography as Gide does. Olinger is in a sense Shillington, of course;
Peter "is" Updike himself as an adolescent with artistic aspirations; and George Caldwell "is" Updike's father, the Shillington
high school teacher. But Updike is not fictionalizing a personal
emotional experience in *The Centaur*: his father has not died,
and he himself has not evolved into a Bohemian artist seeking
a rationale for his vocation but into a novelist who maintains a
respectable middle-class status in spite of his ability to shock.
Yet, as one notes in his essays and short stories, he is drawn
toward factual observation; and his fiction does have a strong
autobiographical bias.

In his later short stories, especially in *The Music School* collection, Updike becomes increasingly involved in the Cubist
tableau-tableau, the problem of self-conscious artistic creation;
but, in *The Centaur*, he has not progressed to that degree of
projected self-awareness as a novelist. Rather, he transfers
the creative problem to Peter, and by this method Updike keeps
himself behind the composition. Since Peter is an artist, it is
natural that he translate his moral-vocational problems into
artistic terms. His effort at a meaningful reconstruction of his
and his father's past, therefore, approximates what Sypher calls
a "facet of the double-consciousness of modern man, the
dédoublement of existential experience."[3] The difference between Updike and Gide (Sypher's model) is that Gide takes
this existential analysis upon himself directly as author-biog-
rapher, while Updike transfers it to his protagonist-narrator.
But still more important is the fact that Updike's artistic and
moral effort, like that of the Cubists, is first purposefully destructive in order to become creative. Both the Cubists and Updike
fracture conventional reality as a prelude to a positive construction of a personal vision. At this point, then, one can begin
to talk about the nature and purpose of Updike's compassionate-
ironic redemptive myth-archetype in *The Centaur*.

III *Varieties of Time*

The novel is saturated by concepts of time and by time consciousness, and the redemption archetype within its Surrealist and Cubist execution is involved in various manifestations of time: in *mythos* (the term to be used to distinguish myth per se from the myth-archetype), *historia* (in its double connotation of the historical past and of fictive narration), and memory (the epistemological vehicle used to mediate between *mythos* and *historia*). But these manifestations do not exhaust the categories of temporality in the story. Updike works with other distinctions of time that are difficult to describe because Western culture does not recognize the nuances, but one can identify them by borrowing ancient Greek terms (appropriately enough) and by demonstrating how they share in the construction of the narrative.

The sense of *aeon*, for example, is prevalent in the early part of the novel. Like the Latin *aeternitas*, it conveys the idea of an enormous length of time, even of immeasurable time. When Caldwell writes a fantastically large number on the board for the benefit of his class in the first chapter, the effect is to induce vertigo. So many zeroes produce the feeling of chaos and infinity; the immensity of time makes the mind reel and search for boundaries that it cannot find. This terrible limitlessness of time creates the infinite context of the novel. It is true that the stress upon *aeon* decreases in the later chapters, but the sense of its power lingers. In fact, the infinite past it represents is gradually transformed into a concern about an infinite future. Although Caldwell has the secular man's cynicism concerning a personal immortality, the mythic element deals directly with that concept. The myth assumes two kinds of immortality: Chiron, who possesses physical immortality, exchanges with the part-human Prometheus, so that the artificer may have eternal life on earth, while Chiron is rewarded with a heavenly immutability. Chiron, therefore, becomes the mythic representative of *aeon*.

The concept of *hora*, by contrast, connotes the immediate and aware present, the instant of *Now* that Caldwell and his son try so desperately to make significant. Characterized by specific traits of space and time, *hora* is the segment of time that is constantly becoming history. It also provides Caldwell with his personal and vocational sense of identity, while his students in their immaturity exist so unconsciously in it that they do not realize how much it controls them. *Hora,* physical time, has a classic brevity in the structure of *The Centaur.* The few days of action in January, 1947, provide the literal, temporal foundation on which the total complex and comprehensive time structure rests. Time moves backward from that brief period, forward beyond it, and through it; and time is transformed into something else through each movement.

Chronos, a third temporal concept, is mechanical time—time passing methodically, sequentially, and measurably. In the first chapter, this time is demonstrated well not only by Caldwell's attempt to beat the bell but also by his wish to be saved by it; for this arbitrary time dictates one's days. Caldwell's creation clock in the initial chapter is a clever teaching device that is also a falsification; it encourages his students to confuse the simplicity of *chronos* with the subtlety of *aeon.* It allows them to control time in the modern empirical manner instead of being made wise by it. Yet the lives of the small-town Pennsylvanians are controlled by *chronos.* Pop Kramer, the grandfather who lives with the Caldwell family, is also old Kronos in the mythic parallel and stands for the domination of the generations by mechanical time. Updike often quotes the time of day throughout the narrative to show the modern obeisance to the artificially imposed minutes and hours of chronologizing. Caldwell is always racing the clock and usually losing; and, at the end of the novel, he as Chiron is even late for the final rendezvous with the death-chariot of Zeus.

Telos is a less spectacular but more crucial quality of time of the novel, for much of the novel's significance is in its teleological action. The concept of *telos* contains the two elements of integrity and consummation. It figures importantly first in Caldwell's lecture to his class: out of the chaos of the immense past, from the accidents of primitive matter and energy, come nonetheless the stubborn, instinctive, and vital gestures toward meaningful life. There *is* a natural movement toward meaning that old Caldwell believes in, and the question that *The Centaur* carries for Peter is whether he can locate a similar consummation and drive toward integrity in his father's suffering existence and in his own sojourn. Is there really a redemptive linearity in the successive preacher-teacher-artist vocations of the Caldwell generations, or is it the circular vanity of Ecclesiastes and Greek myth? Must the mature Peter Caldwell *create* a concrete justification for the life that his father freed him to? Or, to put it another way, is Peter, struggling to express his past and present to his sleeping mistress, a worthwhile step beyond the man who emerged from the immense past, or is he a *de*generation? Or still another possibility may exist: "Out of zero all has come to birth," Updike writes of the Christmas event in a later chapter. In that sense, Christ becomes the focus of *telos*; and even secular man may have to find his redemptive meaning in an interpretation of the Christian Incarnation.

Kairos, a final concept, is existentially decisive time—time measured not by duration but by experiential intensity. It is the relevant moment that redeems the dumb progression of *chronos*, that renders *hora* superfluous, and that justifies the consummating tendency of *telos*. *Kairos* determines the narrative climaxes of *The Centaur*, for Caldwell's struggle, one guesses, is against the impulse to commit suicide. Especially after he learns he does not have the feared stomach cancer, he must rediscover the will to live—for he has already prepared himself to die. The decision to continue living for the sake of his family and his pupils is an agonizing *kairos* moment. Peter's own narration is directed by the *kairos* aspect of time; although he is passively reminiscent during the night of his narration, in bed with his sleeping mistress, the fact of the memory's action working upon him *now* is crucial. He is apparently at some point of personal re-evaluation in his life that will lead to a decision. That decision never appears in the novel; Updike does not carry the story that far—and it is to his credit as an artist that he does not. Rather, he leaves reader and protagonist alike in the suspense and tension of the *kairos* moment that will either force Peter to create his own meaning and identity or leave him in a spiritual paralysis still more crippling than the one that holds him.

The introduction of the young protagonist as involved narrator points to another time-related element. Memory itself in certain chapters of *The Centaur*—and perhaps in all of them, if one sees the whole novel as Peter's recollection— is the dominating fictive device. It is obviously not a category of time, as are *aeon, chronos,* etc.; but it is a structure for encountering and ordering temporality. Memory, or at least the concession to the illusion of memory, directs the formal structure of all fiction, to be sure (otherwise, for example, why tell a story in the past tense?); but Updike has Peter's memory perform a more elemental act. Peter's personal memory in the recollective chapters of *The Centaur* meets myth, a manifestation of man's collective memory (in the Jungian sense) in the other chapters, and deals with it in such a way that the personal memory assumes a surrogate-mythical function. If it is true, as Philip Rieff has declared in *The Triumph of the Therapeutic*, that fiction has supplanted the teaching function of myth, then one can see the new process in operation in this novel.[4] In it, personal memory, or fiction presenting the artistic illusion of personal memory, accomplishes the feat of uniting the subjective and objective aspects of experience that all good literature must somehow do. Myth, emerging from the past as stylized and crystallized memory, meets personal memory coming out of the present (the author's position) into the past (the achieved fiction). Where these two join is where the novel assumes its greatest vitality and most profound meaning, for here is where the subject and object concur in a unified, total artistic experience. Thus memory, much more dynamically than the categorizing mind that classifies *aeon, chronos,* etc., attempts to discipline time by suspending its expressions in recollective narrative form.

Updike commits himself and his protagonist-narrator to the classical epistemological problem of uniting subject and object; but it is also a hermeneutical problem since Peter is trying to articulate for himself, as much as for his mistress, the significance of his past as it affects his present. In the worlds of most novelists, fiction is to myth as fact is to history; and memory would appear to belong to the factual realm. Or, in another formulation, the imagination is to myth what memory is to history. But one learns from the Jungians that the mythic consciousness also has a memory; Updike develops his relationship between memory and myth, feeling his way toward a new, reintegrated experience of time.

Mircea Eliade (in *Cosmos and History*) has argued that primitive man had a terror of history and protected himself from it by the insulating repetitive existence in terms of archetype, myth, and ritual, but that modern man has abandoned the sense of mythic relevance to trust in factuality instead.[5] Updike's fictive mode attempts, through the use of memory in close proximity to myth, to desacralize factuality for modern man—without denying history—and to place myth again in its necessary existential role. Through the same strategy, he empiricizes myth by forcing it under the scrutiny of personal memory. His fiction, therefore, fulfills in good part the sacred and secular functions that Eliade and Rieff demand of narrative prose.

IV Classical Myth and Christian Meaning

Updike uses Classical myth to shape a Christian-informed vision of life. Chiron the centaur as a dual being, part man and part horse, represents the disunity in unity of human nature; he is earthbound, yet possesses an intelligence that makes him vulnerable to longings for the infinite. But the centaurs were also partial divinities, inhabiting a vague superhuman position on the uncertain scale from Titans, gods, and demi-gods down to heroes and mortals. Chiron has immortality and is a mentor of the young heroes; thus he exists in this fashion also on the boundary between creatureliness and godliness. The duality of human nature is carried in the mythic aspect of the novel alone, then, and that in turn acts as the one pole of the myth-realism blend.

Since Chiron is also George Caldwell, he shows another facet of the tension between humanity and divinity that mankind endures. According to this combination, Chiron stands for the eternal and timeless realm to which men have always aspired; Caldwell represents the immanent, time-and-space-bound dilemma that limits men. Furthermore, apart from the mythic dimension altogether, Caldwell himself demonstrates the dual nature of his being. Described emphatically as a secularized Western man of the mid-twentieth century, he cannot be categorized in terms of the orthodox Christian *imago dei* versus Fallen Man, and certainly not in terms of the Protestant *simul justus et peccator*. Instead, Caldwell is aligned to love on the one hand and to death on the other—these mark the extensions and limitations of his being. Behind the comic façade, Caldwell's teaching, his familial and social relationships, and his moral values are inspired by a profound compassion: that is his limitless, charismatic dimension. But, as as scientist and as a physically ill man (or a hypochondriac), he is constantly faced with the imminence of death; and that is the dimension that always recalls him to his humanity.

Every person in *The Centaur* has his corresponding mythic identity or identities, and Peter Caldwell particularly reinforces the dualistic concept inherent in his father's characterization. Because Peter is also Prometheus (a primordial deity, neither god nor man, yet with traits of both), he is ideal for showing the flux of adolescence and the uncertainty of one's vocational choice. Peter, as the fifteen-year-old boy, still retains a degree of the divine innocence of childhood according, for instance, to the Wordsworthian paradigm, although he steadily succumbs to the corruption of the adult world. Or, like Prometheus in the Aeschylean drama (defying Zeus for the sake of mankind and strengthened in his rebellion by the foreknowledge that he and mankind will eventually mature to freedom), Peter is the pivotal figure in the struggle of the generations. In all of this multi-connotation, time is crucial: flux, mutability, the inexorable passing of time mark the substance of human creatureliness, just as its cause and culmination are found in death.

The use of myth can clarify the dilemma of creatureliness in relation to time, but it cannot halt time itself. That realization troubles the adult Peter Caldwell who narrates a good part of the novel; and, to judge from the repeated emphasis in Updike's other stories and novels, this problem fascinates the author himself. Peter (in bed in his Manhattan artist's loft and reminiscing to his sleeping mistress) is caught up in his own attempt to stop time personally and artistically. The two efforts are often hard to distinguish from each other, yet here is another angle of the duality: two Peter Caldwells exist in the novel—the schoolboy and the adult painter; and the tension of the novel develops in large part from the effort to establish a continuity between them. If creatureliness is the result of a compromise between aspiration and reality, Peter as artist expresses the condition quite instructively. He has turned his back on the family professions of preacher and teacher in favor of the artist's freedom—has taken the unlimited risk that should provide total, personal meaning and fulfillment. But he has not discovered or created meaning and satisfaction. He is still young and not yet resigned to mediocrity, but he is already asking the agonizing question of the novel: what went wrong that prevented his self-fulfillment? "*Was it for this that my father gave up his life?*" Peter asks himself during a painful moment of his reappraisal. His effort to suspend those winter days of 1947 through memory, like his "second-rate abstract expressionist" paintings, is a move to create or re-create meaning from the elusive pieces of modern life where meaning is no longer inherent. Son of a scientist, grandson of a minister, and child of the enlightened, empirical generation, Peter in his private and professional desperation returns to mythicizing.

Yet the use of myth is not an escape device (employed to flee an unendurable present) nor a transparent attempt to apotheosize a shabby mundane existence; it is the first step of an evolving esthetic. It is the beginning of a process that moves from theology to science to esthetics, and Peter the narrator defines his life exactly along these lines. The preacher-teacher-artist sequence that he speaks of and the final stage of which he represents exhibits not only a vocational progression or regression (he calls it "the classic degeneration") but also mythological and teleological co-relatives. The preacher-teacher-artist professions are mythologized through Zeus, the divinity; Chiron, the mentor; and Prometheus, the culture-bringer. The direction is from the absolute authoritarianism of the supernatural to the independent rationalism of the empiricist to something not quite articulated. Can a third stage of being dominated by art supersede the previous two? Peter's role would suggest it, and the novel as a whole describes an emergent pattern: man moves from a submissive worship of the divine creator to a scientific effort of scanning creation to the necessary assumption of the creator role himself.

The artist is also the one who suffers the anguish and responsibility of the creator role. The traditional God is no longer taken seriously. As Zeus-Zimmerman, he has his lusts and affairs that are merely overlooked because he has power; but they are not condoned. As the Protestant deity, he is dismissed with the spinster French teacher's banal "*Dieu est très fin*," to which George Caldwell absently responds, "He's a wonderful old gentleman. I don't know where the hell we'd be without Him." But the successor to God, the modern scientist, is also not taken seriously. Chiron as the mythic counterpart enjoys a semi-respect as a sort of lackey to the gods, but Caldwell the science teacher, although he has personally endearing qualities, appears a cheerful fool to his pupils. Against this twofold absurdity, Peter as artist must fashion his own meaning and being. His composition with color, line, proportion, perspective is a means of living metaphorically, of constructing a working model for one's search after personal and ultimate meaning. In other words, when theology and science lose their autonomy and inner structure, art, which is always form, can offer substance. To this end Peter Caldwell wishes to employ his art, and it is the end to which Updike applies his own literary art: the novel both projects and *is* a recovery of the imagination, now that the spirtual and the rational alone have proved inadequate as ways of approaching and ordering existence. And in this effort of the imagination it is, of course, fitting that the author should return to myth as the language of creation.

How then shall Peter Caldwell function in the fearful freedom of his creator role? He must exert the effort, and that is for him more difficult than it sounds; for he suffers from the Kierkegaardian-defined paralysis of the will. Yet his answer is in work. Work involves suffering, and therein another facet of creatureliness is exposed: man is the one who works and suffers for the sake of meaning. In the Greek and Hebrew-Christian myths, suffering has been related to meaning through the motifs of original sin, vocation, and redemption. *Hubris*, the desire to be equal with the gods, is punishable by the necessity of labor (Adam, Sisyphus), suffering, and death. The effects of suffering and death can be relieved only by some expiatory action, but labor becomes an end in itself and even lends a significance to the twin curses of suffering and death.

In Updike's world, suffering and death are present; but original sin as their cause and redemption as the cure are not important. Instead, the gestures of a more elemental guilt and sacrifice inform the structure and meaning of the novel; and both of these, in turn, are balanced by the power of love and by the ordering force of vocation. Guilt in George and Peter Caldwell and in their mythical counterparts grows from the encounter with *Eros* that then becomes, somehow, a conflict with divinity. Thus George Caldwell has withstood the charms of the naked "gym" teacher in the name of traditional morality—on the mythical level, Chiron is tempted to yield to Venus' advances before the thunder of Zeus reminds him of his place. Thus Peter's fumbling explorations with his girlfriend Penny in the 1947 context are to be understood (the catalogue appended to the novel instructs one) as the fateful opening of Pandora's box. Although it is a poor pun, it is an apt symbol of Western attitudes toward sin and sexuality, in which the loss of sexual innocence is akin to the release of qualitative evil itself into the world.

Love, both sexual and familial, does impel guilt in *The Centaur*, but it also leads still deeper into sacrifice; and, in the treatment of this concept, the strategy of the novel structure, especially as seen via the Surrealist-Cubist analogy, becomes quite transparent. The theme of sacrifice appears early in the novel, as George Caldwell explains to his science class that "while each cell is potentially immortal. . . . The strain eventually wears it out and kills it. It dies sacrificially, for the good of the whole." This statement expresses the way in which Caldwell sees his own role in the scheme of life.

The teleological aspect of Caldwell's final decision can now be observed in its personal-mythic context. What happens in the final pages of the novel in literal terms is never clear. Instead of depicting the action in a normal temporal-spatial manner and inviting mythic-symbolic interpretation, Updike presents the mythic dimension but asks the reader to fill in his conclusions about the realistic events. It is a curious post-impressionistic tactic; in Impressionism one would be offered an emotional reaction to an event instead of a description of the event, but in these last pages of *The Centaur* one has, instead of the emotional response, the ultimate "meaning" of the event without a depiction of the event itself. Or more exactly, Updike uses the mythic action as a gloss upon the unwritten realistic narration. Chiron's identity becomes dominant in the concluding chapter. Chiron walks out to the stalled black Buick which he recognizes to be the chariot of Zeus; he pauses for a moment on the edge of a precipice (the abyss of time?)—and then? Updike writes only, after a brief recital in Greek of the Chiron-Prometheus story, that "Chiron accepted death."

V *The Creation of Personal Meaning*

The reader is confronted with the same task that Peter faces: finding meaning in a situation in which sacrifice seems needful but doing so in a context where sacrifice no longer holds religious or cultural relevance. The archetypal model is present, but the contemporary substance is not. Chiron dies to liberate Prometheus from his agony; he is the expiation for

Prometheus' theft of fire from the gods; but Prometheus also provides the welcome opportunity for Chiron to abandon a life he no longer wants. Demythologized, the ending of *The Centaur* suggests that scientific man dies in the context of the old order to make way for the new freedom of the imagination, destroying the limiting modern orthodoxies for the sake of a greater being. But how is Caldwell's sacrifice personally meaningful for Peter? This is the crux of the novel: the teacher has sacrificed himself somehow for the good of the artist; the intellect has prepared the way somehow for the integrating effort of the imagination. Yet the son, the artist, the guardian of the imagination, has not been able to profit from the sacrifice, nor will he ever be able to through passivity or grace alone. Something of ultimate worth has been offered him, but he must still create its value for himself and for his age. Peter has not yet done that; he is attempting at last to create value through his narration in the shared Manhattan loft.

What are the possibilities? The father's sacrifice cannot be rendered significant through a brilliant career of the son; retroactive vindication is meaningless, for it may justify the past but it can do nothing for the present or future. Peter's meaning must be formed in the same anticipation in which his father acted, in a faith in the future which is faith because circumstances do not inspire hope. Prometheus means "forethought," and in the Aeschylean drama the suffering hero on his rock maintains a defiant faith by looking ahead to the prophesied release by his savior Hercules thirteen generations hence. In the novel, Peter returns fourteen years later for a brief visit to Alton and listens to a redemptive praise of his father by Deifendorf-Hercules, the athlete of the old high school days who has become a teacher through Caldwell's influence and who now confesses the value of the profession.

Although Peter cannot vindicate his father's sacrifice through *works*, his creation of personal meaning must develop through *work* and not just through a reliance on the gracious memory of his father's love. Peter's meaning must grow out of the tension of faith and works, out of the tension of past and present, and out of the tension of temporal complexity that the novel depends upon. The force of love must be met by the power of vocation. This emphasis recalls the stress on craftsmanship in the fiction of Willa Cather, Sinclair Lewis, and John Dos Passos; and it has been largely overlooked in discussions of Updike. For Updike—perhaps even more than for Joyce, Proust, Mann, or Faulkner—the past, whether as *historia* or *mythos,* is a point of orientation that must be confirmed and fulfilled in vocation. His own meticulous artistry incarnates the will to create meaning out of one's profession from which an inherent meaning has departed. He believes in work as much as he believes in love, and his fiction is shaped by the desire that modern Americans not only give and find compassion but that they also ground that compassion in tangible, ordered tasks.

The Centaur as a whole has a powerful teleological direction, energized by the stress upon maturity that the body of Updike's fiction illustrates. The main argument against understanding George Caldwell's death as literal suicide is that his mature option is to go on living and suffering. The central significance of Peter's lonely recollection *en deux* is that it is a belated act of maturation. Fourteen years earlier he was Peter-Priapus, a budding phallic god fearing and wondering at his awakening sexual self. Now almost thirty, he decides to conduct a crucial personal inventory as the first step toward true vocation. This, his moment of *kairos,* is the act whereby he begins to refashion himself and his future. Because it is a culminating moment as well, it is also *telos.* Peter now frees himself from the guilt of the past. He takes on the responsibility of faith in the future, faith in his art (hitherto "second-rate") as the vocation-risk that will form his meaning and that will redeem his creatureliness.

CHAPTER 6

Of the Farm:
The Failed Poet and the
Urban Earth Mother

The landscape of love
can only be seen
through a slim windowpane
one's own breath fogs.
—"Erotic Epigrams, I"

I   *Ellipsis in the Country*

IF fiction is in part the art of leaving things significantly unsaid, Updike succeeds admirably in his fourth novel, *Of the Farm*. Once more the book reviewers were willing to allow that the technique was perfectly controlled, but they argued again that the subject matter was neither significant nor especially interesting. A weekly news magazine, with typical clichéd hyperbole, likened the book to the composition of a painting on a pinhead; and a good critic, John Thompson, decided in *The New York Review of Books* that whatever truths the novel was masking were not worth uncovering.[1]

Admittedly, Updike moves closer to the artistic-esoteric in *Of the Farm* than in his previous fiction, but the rewards are correspondingly greater for those who strive to appreciate the book's form; for it is the best integrated of his first four novels. Conflict, complication, climax—the old components of the well-made plot—are so constantly and intensely present that they subordinate the normal mechanics of storytelling. It is not that plot has been minimized in the interest of some other narrative emphasis but that the ingredients of action have been drastically simplified to provide what one could call a fictive transparency toward actual modern living. *Of the Farm* is a radically pared-down work that succeeds by virtue of its technical concentration and ellipsis, but it is not a long short story, as one critic defined it; its accomplishment of scope and depth supersedes the short-story potential.

The protagonist is Joey Robinson, a thirty-five-year-old Manhattan advertising consultant who has smothered poetic aspirations and who visits his widowed mother over a weekend on her eastern Pennsylvania farm. In his company are his recently acquired second wife Peggy and her precocious eleven-year-old son Richard. Joey is a literary relative of Harry Angstrom and Peter Caldwell. Like the Caldwell family, the Robinsons moved from Olinger, at the insistence of the strong-willed mother, to a farm in the country against the wishes of the father (here again a high school science teacher) and the son. Like Rabbit Angstrom, Joey is hypersensitive, unstable, and dominated by his mother; and he suffers the resultant sex-and-security complications with his women. The difference is that Joey, a Harvard graduate and a qualified success in his vocation, is respectable middle-class.

A main purpose of the visit is to give Joey's ailing mother and his new wife a chance to know each other better, but the weekend is not very successful. The women are alternately hostile and overfriendly; at times, they are defensive in their attitudes toward Joey; at other times, suspicious of his loyalties. Joey himself has to tangle not only with the sparring females but also with the ghosts of his past. The memories of his dead father, of his first wife, and of their three children now living in Canada are revived by the old familiar surroundings and by photographs; and these memories release Joey's suppressed feelings of remorse and guilt.

Very little significant overt action occurs: Joey mows the overgrown field with the family tractor; he and his mother take a trip to the local supermarket; the two of them attend a Lutheran church service on Sunday morning. Instead of dynamic action, the novel is filled with conversation and description. The climax, if it can be called that, takes place on Sunday noon when old Mrs. Robinson, excited by the tensions of the visit, suffers a heart seizure on the way home from church. She is put to bed, the town doctor examines her briefly, and the son and family plan the return trip to New York that evening in spite of her illness.

II   *The Crucial X and Vital Incongruity*

A few years ago during a television interview, Updike remarked that he conceived the design of one of his novels as the figure of an "X." The concept fits this novel and reveals the visual bias of his creative technique—the surviving graphic orientation that, while certainly not anti-intellectual, demands of the reader that he perceive *Gestalt* and not only verbalized ideas. The "X" serves as the model for metaphors of intersection and interaction, as the representative structure of characterization, as the unifying figure in the manipulation of time and space, and as both the integer and unknown quality of the story's problem.

The geometrically fashioned metaphors in *Of the Farm* seem whimsical at first, belabored Donne-like conceits; but they have a precise place in the book's scheme. Not only the "X," but squares, rhomboids, triangles, circles, curves, and angles frequently inform the imagery. Through the lines of the highway, the patterns of the fields and the farmhouse, and the contours of the women in his life, the protagonist is made to see and describe through a vocabulary of formal shapes and measurements. It is as if, against the loss of the old societal order, the author imposes a tentative artificial order of mathematical forms.

In the most general sense, the story is "X"-formed through its stress on intersection and interaction. The particular import of this emphasis may be a bit difficult to see since the energy of any piece of fiction depends upon interaction of people and events. The difference is that, while in most novels the interaction is a kind of anatomy that supports the thematic and cultural overlay (what humanist and social-oriented critics talk about), such interaction in *Of the Farm* is a simultaneous means and end. For example, the total act of the story is to depict literally the crux, the "X," of Joey's life. It is the intersection of his experience to date. The return to the old farm in these particular and peculiar circumstances brings together the two divergent lines of his existence: his childhood ideals, his first wife and three children, his stable sojourn versus the disillusionment of adulthood, the passion and vulgarity of the second marriage, and his essentially romantic new mode of life. These lines meet at the farm in the encounter with the mother (this meeting is the center of the "X"); then they cross and move off in two new directions. The farm, the mother, and the old life still hanging on must be sloughed off; and the passionate new life must be embraced with fuller commitment. The lengthening arms of the "X" now recede farther from each other, and Joey must choose and live conclusively with his choice.

Or, in another sense native to Updike's imagery and representative of the novel as a whole, the chiasmic pattern is elemental-sexual. The prone and outstretched female forms the "X," and to make love with her is to perform something "crucial" that touches the mysterious core of being. Hence Updike's concern with the convergence of the woman's thighs and with pudenda: here is the center of the "X" where decisive experience occurs. The woman as symbol of the mystery of being to be plumbed is a basic metaphor of the novel, and the "X" figure gives it an underlying stylized simplicity. In the Sunday morning church scene a depiction of the cross (an "X") precedes the sermon on woman's place in God's creation as both the security and secret of being, while the whole scene is itself another intersection, another blending of divergent strands in the book.

Recalling an ecstatic moment of the affair with Peggy before their marriage—a lover's morning in the city complete with music, fine weather, and the revealed flesh—Joey says, "I was transfixed.... I felt my heart pinned at the point where the snow and Bach and her bathing intersected." That passage is one of the epitomizing metaphors of the novel. The redemption of significant moments out of the plurality of experience provides the genuine, if precarious, spiritual foundation of Updike's fictive world. It is precarious because it must constantly be created anew, without the help of tradition (although it exists within tradition); but it is genuine because it wishes to support whatever of value survives in the shifting middle-class civilization. Yet the metaphor in this particular setting also introduces a crucial act; for this meeting is the last between Joey and Peggy unless he agrees to get a divorce. The need for decision creates meaning, and the sense of convergence that the "X"-shaped metaphor contains stresses the concentration of being into a decisive moment that determines the meaning. In other words, the technical shape of Updike's fiction creates the shape of its meaning.

If the geometric properties of the "X" form lead to such

baroque analysis, the algebraic implications direct one toward more intellectualized possibilities. The "X" structure signifies an unknown quality (not the quantity, naturally, of mathematics but the quality of symbolic logic) and a functional interchangeability. Joey's weekend at the farm is an effort to uncover the secret of life's failures, much in the manner of Peter Caldwell's personal inventory in his artist's loft. The secret in *Of the Farm* is in the land, in Joey's past, his women, and his vocation—and all these subtly join during the two-day visit to elicit paradoxical understanding and to send him back to the city with a unique freedom. Ultimately, the unknown quality is Joey himself; and he gains identity only in relation to others. In this respect, the analogy of the "X" as an interchangeable symbol is helpful. Joey combined with his mother and later with Joan have produced only wrong solutions; but, with Peggy, his problems are being solved correctly. Even in love relationships, one remains inauthentic, unidentified, until one locates himself in the company of the truly sympathetic lover. That Joey has done, and that is why he needs Peggy so desperately.

The novel depends vitally on the "X" format but no less importantly on a fundamental incongruity that develops through setting, character confrontations, and fictive mood and tone. The mere juxtaposition of city and country supplies a basic disharmony of locales. The Manhattanites on the Pennsylvania farm do not fit, and flashes of description reveal their displacement, such as the glance at Peggy, barefoot with painted red toenails, hoeing clumsily in the garden soil, or Joey himself, now a smooth Madison Avenue "adman," mowing the shaggy rural field. The incongruity grows through the depicted inability of the mother and the new daughter-in-law to commune, although they can communicate, and through the precociousness of the eleven-year-old stepson Richard, who speaks like a self-conscious college freshman and whose language jars against the natural environment.

Strangest of all is the dissonant effect of the lush, evocative, lyrical prose joined to the blunt discovery of normally private areas. Joey can speak quite crudely to his wife and joke about her used Tampax while he is rhapsodizing about her beauty and about the old charm of the countryside. The gross comment performs the trick of heightened contrast, but the whole phenomenon illustrates Updike's artistic method in almost all of his fiction. The mundane, even the hitherto unspeakable (if any of that remains in the post-censorship era), are rendered selectively significant because of the author's persuasion that life, and therefore art, consist of the acknowledgment and utilization of the trivial, a coming to terms with the daily little things.

In *Of the Farm* the incongruity extends to the diction itself, which includes "disharmony," "distention," "seeking equilibrium," "disproportionately," "incongruously." Many other aspects of the story which give a jarring tone to the novel are fashioned from incongruity: the discussion of God while eating baloney, Joey's wearing a coolie hat to mow the field, Peggy dressed in a mauve polka-dot bikini in the conservative country. Incongruity is the passive side of conflict; and, through this exhaustive use of the incongruous, conflict, like the other formal elements of action, becomes determinative without ever really contributing to the story line.

III   *The Woman and the Land*

Updike works precariously in *Of the Farm* with natural and artistic forms that threaten at any moment to explode and disintegrate, but he also counteracts that impulse with a pervasive trick of metaphor that re-establishes unity. A "gimmick" exists in each Updike novel: the futurism of *The Poorhouse Fair,* the present tense of *Rabbit, Run,* the myth-realism combination of *The Centaur.* Although this device is less spectacular in *Of the Farm,* it appears in the analogy of woman and land. The analogy matures along the three closely related lines of sexuality, fertility, and security. The locus of each pole of the analogy is specific: the woman is always Peggy, and the land is always the old parental farm property, while the other women of the story are antagonistic contrasts to the image. Joan, Joey's first wife, appears as a cold and distant female (she now lives in Canada), even though she has borne Joey three children; and old Mrs. Robinson, Joey's mother, has a brittle barrenness about her person, although she is most intimately connected with the farm. The parental farmland, in turn, has an exclusive connotation for Joey. In his mind it stands apart from the actual sameness of the surrounding fields and pastures and maintains itself against the steady invasion of new highways and creeping suburbia. Although Updike moves from one pole

of the metaphor to another, the obvious interest centers upon
Peggy: she is a city girl (although originally from Nebraska—
farming country) whose physical and emotional nature invites
the analogy of the land. She is big, broad, sensual, impulsive—
and voluptuous, a word that Updike carefully avoids, describes
her well.

The sexual chords of woman and land are sounded early and
echo throughout the book. The intercourse image is dominant,
and Joey is the husband in the double sense: he is the keeper
of the woman and of the soil. He muses, "My wife is wide, wide-
hipped and long-waisted, and, surveyed from above, gives an
impression of terrain, of a wealth whose ownership imposes
upon my own body a sweet strain of extension; entered, she
yields a variety of landscapes." In the scene described earlier,
Joey mows the hourglass-shaped piece of grass "in one ecstatic
straight thrust, up the middle"; and, during the same afternoon's
work, "The tractor body was flecked with foam and I, rocked
back and forth on the iron seat shaped like a woman's hips . . .
excited by destruction, weightless, discovered in myself a swell-
ing which I idly permitted to stand, thinking of Peggy."

The fertility imagery is connected with Peggy, with the land,
and with blood and rain. Joey returns from the supermarket to
see his wife, bikini-clad, hoeing the garden, and says, "We
stopped the car beneath the pear tree whose surviving limbs
disproportionately put forth the full tree's burden of fruit."
By metaphoric association, the ripeness of the tree enhances
the woman's fertility. Joey, in fact, in a moment of intense love
for Peggy, thinks impulsively that he would like to make her
pregnant. Later on, as he finishes mowing the hourglass plot
of grass, the rain begins to fall; and Updike describes the scene
again through sexual-fertile images that invite transposition:
"And now the rain, having taken one last breath, sighed and
subsided into the earth, gently at first, sweetly . . . then with
such steady relaxed force, pattering on my hat, soaking my
thighs, that the closed flowers bobbed beneath the drumming
and the grass, whipped, gleamed."

The woman-land metaphor works to give Joey his needed
comfort and security against the pain of his lost children and
first wife and against the threat of the past that his mother and
the farm somehow darkly embody. He comes from tense dialogue
with his mother and from the fields to the seclusion of the bed-

room and his wife. "You never should have left your mother's womb," Peggy tells him in bed, and he agrees. Like Rabbit Angstrom, who wants to "bury himself" in his mistress, Joey uses his wife's body as psychological-physical escape.

The structure of the book thus develops skillfully the problematical situation of characters. Incongruity of setting, language, and personality and the answering resolution of incongruity via metaphor surround the division and attempted reconciliation in the protagonist's life. His existence is incongruous, even paradoxical; he is the small-town mother's boy turned Manhattanite, the would-be poet become Madison Avenue consultant, the husband and father who has abandoned those he loved for a lesser life. Now he is condemned to making the best of his choice by forcing artificial combinations to work. The land versus his second wife and what he had and was versus that to which he has committed himself must now be molded into some kind of unity; the metaphoric attempt at unity indicates the intensity of Joey's need, even though the integration does not function on any literal basis. In this sense also, conflict as a fictional end in itself, instead of as an ingredient of plot, serves its purpose; for this conflict is not one that leads to resolution but one that remains a fact of existence. Insoluble dilemmas are the order of the day, and fiction such as Updike's accommodates them by fixing them in positions of artistic clarity.

IV   *Anguish, Freedom, and Responsibility*

The novel is also the dramatized moment of a philosophical tenet: the concept of the paradox of existential freedom. Updike prefixes the story with the familiar quotation from Sartre: "Consequently, when, in all honesty, I've recognized that man is a being in whom existence precedes essence, that he is a free being who, in various circumstances, can want only his freedom, I have at the same time recognized that I can want only the freedom of others." If *Rabbit, Run* exudes a Kierkegaardian *angst*, the fear of nil beneath a surface of senseless being, *Of the Farm* deals with anguish in its existential setting as the intellectual-emotional result of the tension between individual freedom and social responsibility.

Updike is not necessarily using the quotation from Sartre as a text for his story; in fact, he neatly underscores the weakness of the existence-before-essence stance when he has Joey cynically state that "Truth is constantly being formed from the solidification of illusions." Nevertheless, Joey is caught in the existential predicament, stretched taut amidst the many demands around him and pinned precisely (to use Updike's own image) at the intersection of the conflicts. He has made his choice, and perhaps it was the existential one: to leave wife and children for the woman and for the liberation he thought he desired. Now, at the farm, he is faced with another decision, one more subtle but hardly less significant: he must decide whether to sell the farm after his mother's death and thereby to free himself still further from the burden of the past, to deny his essence in favor of existence in another dimension. True, he never does make the decision unequivocally—he lets things ride instead—but, in leaving his mother and returning to the city, he decides in effect after all against the past and toward an undefined, or ill-defined, future.

Even if his decision were clearly rendered, the conflict of responsibility and freedom that causes anguish, and the other situations that aggravate it, would still remain. Joey still loves Joan, as he confesses to his mother, and he also suffers from the loss of his children; but, on the other hand, leaving them for Peggy has been his step to freedom. The paradox of existential freedom, then, is that one never becomes unconditionally free. One is always free only from and to something or someone; the condition that promotes anguish is the responsibility to past and future that remains. Updike's main contribution through the novel to the understanding of modern freedom is his detailed presentation of the anguish involved.

V   *Das ewig Weibliche*

The godless City of God, the fruitless search for the Holy Grail, and the myth of heaven and earth seem to clarify well Updike's first three novels; but he is not as mythologically inclined in *Of the Farm*. What one does find is an ironic version of the myth of the eternal female, as it relates to the earth mother (who is also the archetypal terrible mother), the *femme fatale*, and the unattainable woman. All of these are contained in the Eve archetype (Eve is the focus of the Lutheran pastor's sermon), and all of them gain significance in their effect upon the male.

Digressing a moment into summarizing graphic analogies, one might describe *The Poorhouse Fair* as a solid globe suspended in space (a static, self-contained little world); *Rabbit, Run* as a longitudinal line that appears straight but comes round to meet itself again; *The Centaur* as two overlapping vertical lines; and *Of the Farm* as two triangles that touch at an apex. This last image should not cancel the intersection image described earlier but enhance it; for the most important triangle is the female element. Its angles represent Peggy, Joey's mother, and Joan. The other, the male triangle, is formed by Richard, Dean McCabe (Peggy's ex-husband), and Joey's dead father. Joey (once again the pervasive "X" figure) is suspended in, and as, the double apex; and the male triangle threatens his already uncertain masculinity. His eleven-year-old stepson, with his precociousness and casual mastery of life, offers him no vicarious return to innocence or even a chance to play the father. The academician McCabe forces an added worry upon Joey: did McCabe divorce Peggy, instead of vice versa, so that Joey somehow has been duped? And the frequent memory of Joey's father, dead only a year, is no comfort; for he too was dominated by the female and offers no model but rather prefigures too well what Joey's destiny might be.

Joey therefore flees the masculine challenge and absorbs himself in the feminine complex, much as Rabbit Angstrom did by refusing to compete in the middle-class, adult world. A dangerous maneuver for Joey, it traps him in a disintegrating kind of union with the three women from which he must painfully extricate himself. His mother, curiously perhaps, has embodied all three of the archetypal forms: she has been the earth mother ("of the farm"), *femme fatale*, and unattainable woman for him. Her role as earth mother was artificial and grew from her insistence upon rural life, for she wanted the farm and forced country living upon her unwilling husband and son. It is an ironic situation, for the proximity to the soil produced no fertility. Since husband and son did not want to farm, the rural life has been a barren waste and a frustration. Mrs. Robinson was also the seductive female for her young son. One of Joey's vivid childhood recollections is of the desirable mother: "I seemed to be in bed, and a tall girl stood above me, and her hair came loose from her shoulder and fell forward filling the air with a swift liquid motion, and hung there, as a wing edged with light, and enclosed me in a tent as she bent lower to deliver her good-night kiss." In that sense, she was already the unattainable woman for him; and that role is reinforced by her wish for his vocation, that he become a poet. Joey has failed in being one; he has failed to please her and feels rejected by her.

As a result, he has sought his special kind of mother-surrogate in Joan and has suffered the same kind of defeat. His first wife was also aloof but ambitious for him; she was another woman on a pedestal whom he could not reach. But, with Peggy, Joey has at last the chance for a true marriage. The situation is fundamentally ironic, and the price that he must pay is very high. The irony resides in the fact that Peggy, the *femme fatale,* the "vulgar woman" who has also slept around, is the only one who has the instincts and understanding of a good wife. The eternal female of myth (*das ewig Weibliche*), with her seductive, destructive propensities, is here the one who heals and fulfills.

In the light of this background, the weekend at the farm can be seen as a decisive struggle. On the surface, it provides opportunity for Peggy and Joey's mother to become acquainted. Beneath, it is a fight for Joey between the two women. Although it is unjust to cast old Mrs. Robinson as the conscious villainess, she does use all the weapons in her arsenal—memories, maternal respect, family pride, religion, age, illness—to get what she wants. She wants really only a vindication of her way and interpretation of life, but that is what Joey cannot allow her; for to do so would destroy his own future. The conflict is, in a sense, D. H. Lawrence's *Sons and Lovers* all over again; but Updike's protagonist finds the woman who can outcharm the mother. Peggy is the seductress who helps Joey free himself not only from the "terrible mother" who kills her children with over-possessiveness, but also from the unattainable female who generates guilt about sexuality and male identity. For Peggy is a genuine earth mother, not an artificial one; as seductress or *femme fatale,* she leads Joey to the death of his old self, it is true, but also into the first full and satisfying relationship of his life. "I'm the first woman he's ever met who was willing to let him be a man," Peggy tells 'the old woman in anger; and, while that cliché justifies the cruel divorce and remarriage, it is also true.

Peggy is also the archetypal Eve, and the young Lutheran pastor strengthens that identification through his sermon. One should not take the homily altogether seriously—Updike has a penchant for satirizing theologians and preachers— and this Sunday morning discourse takes too many unwitting comic turns to be meant as genuine religious proclamation. The sermon, however, does neatly outline Joey's dilemma and his possible solution. Eve is the helpmeet, the creature who draws man away from his preoccupation with infinity and death and who incites him to an act of faith—his acknowledgment of his humanity by living with compassion and kindness. Peggy is and does these things for Joey. She could be called inferior to him, as the pastor insists that women must be (Joey's mother says that Peggy is stupid); but she is also his superior since she has come to terms with existence in a way that none of the others has by utilizing the power of her womanliness. If she is the secondary temptress (after Lilith?) who has destroyed, by passion, the innocence of Eden, she is also equipped and eager to support her man in the world that opens up beyond the flaming sword. The act of faith she leads him to commit is identical with the step toward freedom that secular man must take. Joey must cut himself off from the security of the past (the mother, the land), assume the anguish of responsibility, and immerse himself in creating new meaning out of personal relationships. The eternal woman, therefore, offers a tangible mode of being that the metaphysics of infinity does not.

VI *Continuity and Closure*

Through this interpretation, the conclusion of the novel becomes clear. Joey, having made the decision against the mother, offers a final gesture of kindness. He has mowed the field (and thus symbolically put his past in order) and must return to the city, for there his future and freedom wait. But he leaves his slowly dying mother with the kindness of an illusion, with a compassionate lie. "When you sell my farm, don't sell it cheap. Get a good price," his mother tells him from her bed. The farm is important. It is the earnest of her life's meaning, the solid symbol of her identity in a world of absolutes fading fast. Joey writes, "I must answer in our old language, our only language, allusive and teasing, that with conspiratorial tact declared nothing and left the past apparently unrevised"—*apparently* unrevised, but everything has changed. Joey replies, in the last words of the book, "*Your* farm?... I've always thought of it as our farm." He willingly plays out the charade, not to deceive but to comfort, and that is an act of his new, complex responsibility.

The novel contains other fascinating aspects that can be mentioned only briefly. Updike works with an orchestration of the four natural elements—earth, air, fire, water—throughout the narrative to give the story still another kind of fundamental structure and unity. He uses ghost imagery as a motif to signify the intangible influence of the past and the omnipresent sense of death in the book. He plays with metaphors and with games of vorticism (as in the bedtime story he tells to Richard about the frog who went so far inside himself that he disappeared) as part of the visual-art interest that reveals another imaginative view of infinity and death. He employs a risky academic diction ("susurrous," "pronation," "tesserae," "homunculus") and yet manages to catch the flavor of authentic Pennsylvania German speech.

For all its richness, *Of the Farm* is certainly not flawless. In fact, the proliferation of design, image, and motif, in spite of the small cast of personae and the simplicity of action, threatens both the reader's receptivity and the book's total unity. Updike overloads the circuits and forces the novel genre to do more than it can. This extremely self-conscious fiction fashions nuance out of nuance, and the danger is not that the intricacies and complexities may be exposed as trivia in disguise but that they implode, as it were, the narrative format and make it difficult to encounter the story on any single level. The book is so tightly compressed, hard and glittering in so many directions like a cut and polished diamond, that the reader can admire it but hardly find an entry to see inside. Truly an artist's novel, it must be intensely studied in terms of its unique and skillful execution if it is to be appreciated.

CHAPTER 7

The Music School:
Strange Chords and Strained Cords

When you look	kool uoy nehW
into a mirror	rorrim a otni
it is not	ton si ti
yourself you see,	,ees uoy flesruoy
but a kind	dnik a tub
of apish error	rorre hsipa fo
posed in fearful	lufraef ni desop
symmetry.	.yrtemmys

—"Mirror"

I Reflections of Reality

UPDIKE'S third collection of short stories, *The Music School,* represents a continuation of his characteristic artistry but also a radical departure in theme and mood from his previous fiction. Published in 1966 and containing twenty stories originally written for *The New Yorker* between 1962 and 1966, *The Music School* projects a brittleness and a neurotic insight into adult problems that the earlier collections only suggested. But Updike's personal vision has not moved off-center in any way; he has, in effect, done what the critics have been suggesting that he do: abandoned the boyhood context and moved on to the more painful and immediate actuality of urban and suburban sophistication. Olinger has yielded further to Manhattan and New England; and the high school locale and young-marrieds milieu give way to the dissection of ailing and failed marriages among the worldly-wise. The characters have grown older and are now mostly in their thirties; they are professionally and economically successful but at some impasse in their personal and social lives. The adultery motif is stronger than any other throughout the book.

111

Updike's style has also expanded to include the shifting emphasis. The stories have become more "scenic" and more inclined toward the essay format. They are scenic in that the author often withdraws the participating "I" and observes with a new, cool detachment; they are essay-like in the exhibited tendency away from traditional fictive dramatization and toward discursive—or at least meditative—analysis. It seems occasionally in this collection that Updike is too aware for his vehicle, that his perceptivity has moved beyond the craft of his storytelling, and that this uneven development has tempted him to declare instead of insinuate. His technique is quite legitimate, for the objective statements occur within the framework of interior monologues or scaffoldry of setting; yet it becomes apparent that Updike, no longer satisfied with the limitations that the traditional short-story format places upon him, is constantly searching for extensions of the form compatible with his intuitions.

Many of these tales culminate not in the recognition of grace (as in *The Same Door*) nor of comforting design (as in *Pigeon Feathers*) but, instead, in a melancholy realization of failed or missed moments that could have changed one's life. A sense of "too late" and a corresponding mood of regret and sometimes remorse indwells *The Music School* stories. But the situations of loss neither rise to the nobility of tragedy nor sink into the paralysis of despair. Grief is something one learns to accommodate and assimilate, and the significant moment of many of the stories is the prosaic step of the protagonist toward learning to live with his loss. These are tales of adjustment and compromise; the artistic accomplishment is in making credible and absorbing the recovery of a personal equilibrium. Although the gift of grace is not emphasized, the fact that one *can* effect a recovery, that one can go on after all, is a gift in itself that the veteran of life accepts as such; therefore, in an important way, the people in *The Music School* move through alienation into a healing participation in things.

Unlikely though it may seem, a number of these stories do offer a moral advance beyond the earlier ones. Updike is developing a fictional technique and content that signal the end of a lingering Romanticism (the belief that life consists of a series of climaxes), that articulate the logical conclusion to Realism (the belief that art follows life down to the irrelevant, nonartistic details), and then present the outlines of the next step. That next step is the result of Updike's conviction that one can select moments from the flux of normal existence (or what passes for normal) and transform them into valid metaphors of meaning by extending them backward into time through memory, downward psychologically into myth, and forward "eschatologically" with a hope that the future will somehow clarify one's present failed existence.

That step is a far cry from Realism and Naturalism, yet it is not all that new; for Henry James and James Joyce had similar intentions. The difference is that Updike depends in *The Music School* less crucially on the inherent qualities of memory and myth and much more on the evocative power of his own language. His metaphors become self-identical and self-contained, which is to say that, instead of reflecting some extrinsic reality, they project mainly themselves. The author's method is to create metaphors of metaphors—which does not mean that his fiction is twice removed from reality. Instead, a reciprocal cancellation process occurs whereby, as when one places two mirrors face to face, one achieves an illusion of infinity and therewith a model *for* infinity. This achievement is the reward for the artist's faith in pure form. When he pursues the potential of imaginative language into its deeper dimensions, he is blessed with a sudden reappearance of reality that the frontal assault would never compel.

II *The Maples' Marriage*

Ten of the stories in *The Music School* have to do with marriage relationships (eleven, if one includes the premarital situation of "The Morning") that are clouded by approaching or realized divorces or affairs or both. Two tales, "Giving Blood" and "Twin Beds in Rome," return to Richard and Joan Maple of "Snowing in Greenwich Village." They have moved to New England, they now have four children, and their nine years of matrimony have nurtured mistrust and discord. In the first story, they are on their way to Boston to donate blood at a hospital for Joan's ailing aunt; and they fill the thirty-mile drive with accusations against each other. But, once in the hospital, the shared experience of giving blood draws them together and repairs the breach. Afterwards they eat lunch together like a pair of lovers at a roadside restaurant, but that mood is broken when Richard discovers he hasn't enough money to pay for the meal. The animosity returns, and they are estranged once more.

The return into the past is not just the nostalgic attempt to capture a childhood security, as the characters in the Olinger stories often strive to do. Instead, the relative vulnerability and innocence of the couple as they face a harmless but elemental operation reduces them to a momentary childhood that helps them see afresh themselves and their marriage. Updike emphasizes the childhood images: Richard sees the two of them as Hansel and Gretel; he fights the impulse to giggle; they recount their adolescent diseases; Joan's hair seems to Richard as if combed by her mother; Joan thinks the plastic sacks filled with their blood look like doll pillows. These thoughts constitute not only personal memory but a measure of collective memory also. "Mr. and Mrs. Maple were newly defined to themselves," Updike writes. The unique act of being bled, bringing them close to the mystery of their own bodies, renews the freshness and clarity and yet the mystery of all childhoods, of the pre-initiation period of life. This return to the past is moral in that it gives the worldly-wise Maples a sudden chance to see their contentious and bored adulthood through naïve eyes and effects their own condemnation of their present selves by their past ones.

The psychological deepening of the fictive moment into myth occurs through the sacrifice motif. Although the blood-giving is essentially an act of compassion (reluctant compassion on Richard's part), Updike weights the description with sacrificial images. Most directly, he refers to "the mystical union of the couple sacrificially bedded together." Blood and sacrifice have always been closely connected in human religiosity, and that combination, even in the secular setting, allows the story its mythic awareness. Yet, because it is a secular context, the myth becomes demythologized at once. Why are the Maples sacrificing and to whom? In their profane and empty suburban world they are engaged in a totally immanent ritual. No god exists to be manipulated via expiation, no natural force is to be appeased except death, but also no guilt exists except that which the childhood memory uncovers.

The sacrifice, therefore, beyond the superficial mechanics of donating literal blood to a distant relative, becomes a sacrifice of themselves to each other. Since that is a possible interpretation of marriage in the Western Christian tradition, the sacrifice does not seem all that momentous. And yet, in a society that has abandoned the transcendent realm, the organic quality of marriage—the mutual sacrifice resulting in a greater something, in a spiritual union—also fades; and remaining is a liaison of mutual destruction. The Maples' being bled simultaneously images the enervating effect they have on each other. The marriage effort has become the attempted sacrifice of the other to oneself, and thus the sacrificial subject and object have shifted. The underlying and perhaps even subliminal realization of this struggle for personal assertion shapes the psychological and mythical facets of the narrative moment.

Updike extends that moment into the future by projecting the motifs of childhood and sacrifice into a coherent pattern of judgment. Toward the end of the story, the Maples have eased, because of the hospital experience, into a lovers' mood at the restaurant; but Richard dispels it when, finding only a dollar in his wallet, he succumbs to a self-pitying rage at the frustrating ineffectiveness of his suburban existence that his near-empty billfold represents. The childish action ruins the precarious illusion of affection, but Joan does not respond in kind. "We'll both pay," she says quietly; and, although she refers to the restaurant bill, the meaning applies still better to their marriage. They *will* both pay, both sacrifice, if they stay together; and that payment is their self-inflicted condemnation. This eschatological direction substitutes for the traditional climax of action. The Maples can look forward not to the gift of grace but only to their intrinsic judgment. That is a bleak prospect indeed, but it is an honest and convincing assessment of a current American marital sickness. It is not tragic; it is not comic; it is the way it is—but Updike renders that truth truthful not by documentation but by imaginative evocation. He creates, by metaphorical indirection, a metaphysics of ennui.

"Twin Beds in Rome," which continues the marital dilemma of the Maples, suggests another solution beyond the punishment of continuing in an unhappy union. Richard and Joan (no mention is made of their children) have traveled to Rome in an effort to give their faltering marriage a salutary change; but what happens there is not amorous adventure. On their first full day, they take a sightseeing walk; and, since Richard's shoes hurt him, he buys new ones. Then he has a stomach cramp so severe that they must return to the hotel, where he naps for an hour and recovers. Somehow the brief illness becomes the event that relaxes the tension of the marriage; although it does not reconcile them, it liberates them individually. They enjoy their newly felt personal freedom and their Roman vacation, and at the end Richard begins to fall in love with his wife again.

"Twin Beds in Rome" commences where "Giving Blood" concludes. One notices especially the progression of the judgment motif: the judgment has been made; the couple accepts it; and, in the act of acceptance, each suddenly finds a new freedom *from* the other. The act gives new import to the sacrifice theme. Now, it seems, when the Maples are ready to offer up the marriage itself, they locate a new value in the marriage union. What has been wrong, one sees in retrospect, is that the Maples, with typical modern introspection, objectified their marriage and transformed it into a thing with a problematic life of its own, instead of recalling that marriage is a most intimate meeting of persons designed to enhance and deepen love rather than destroy it. They have sought the solution to their dilemma in the mechanics of matrimony as an institution, rather than in a checking of their own failings as partners in the sacrament, but Updike finally has them see each other as vital metaphors of themselves instead of continuing the search for an illusory objective second image. This metaphor of metaphor in action leads the couple out of a marital dead end into personal freedom.

The title also hints at their progress: they have twin beds for the first time, here in the city of sensuality and passion, and forfeit the comforting habit of the double bed. Richard's illness, next, is the mild trauma that both signals and precipitates the liberation act. He is the weaker of the pair, and his hypersensitivity and grown-up childishness define their union; Joan indulges him and confirms her position of strength, while he employs her as the object of his tantrums and other irresponsibilities. Each needs the other to persist in his private neurosis, and the marriage is indeed based on a sickness.

Richard's psychosomatic stomach-ache becomes the fitting irritation that frees them. Like their marriage, the pain is a nagging and not quite definable one that exhausts Richard, just as the marital liaison saps both their energy. Just how the incident of the cramp releases the Maples to their individual freedom is unclear, and apparently the couple does not understand it either. But it does serve as the first event that takes their intent vision away from themselves and their entrapment; once they begin exploring Rome, they are drawn out of themselves, away from their preoccupation, and into a relatively healthy humor.

As Updike writes in "Giving Blood," "Romance is, simply, the strange, the untried," and that is what the Maples, without dwelling on it self-consciously, experience in Rome—or at least Richard does. Now that his wife, "released from the tension of hope," has become free and girlishly desirable once more, her husband begins to want her again. But that is the end of the story, and this conclusion can be variously interpreted.

III "The Music School"

This tentative approach to the inevitable sorrows and losses of daily life is expressed in an image from the title story of the collection, "The Music School," in which the hero sees and hears "hints of another world, a world where angels fumble, pause, and begin again." The faint Aristotelian-mimetic quality about the quotation reveals how remote Updike and his fictive environment are from the ideal world. Updike's people are not angels, and the ideal that the concept of angels elicits is lost in the pedestrian detail of pragmatic striving and petty strife. The invitation to imitate an ideal reduces itself, therefore, to the contemplation of esthetic models themselves (the metaphor of metaphor) and no longer extends to a faith in some ordering, encompassing mind of God. Thus the "music school," where the young innocents play groping tunes on instruments they cannot handle, is not an image of divine harmony but a pathos-ridden paradigm of the exercises their elders practice in learning life's notes.

The music school is life. The thirtyish father, suspended in adultery and possible divorce, actually does participate through his daughter in her initiation into the musical mysteries; but the experience does not guide him toward any knowledge of universal design or metaphysical verities—only back in upon himself: "Vision, timidly, becomes percussion, percussion becomes music, music becomes emotion, emotion becomes—vision. Few of us have the heart to follow this circle to its end." The story itself progresses according to this pattern; for, in the first section, the protagonist describes a change in the Communion ritual as he had heard it described by a young priest the night before; that is the "vision." In the second section, he refers to a startling newspaper item: a casual acquaintance of his, a computer expert, has been mysteriously shot and killed; this is the "percussion" of life. In the third section, "percussion becomes music": he depicts the basement of the Baptist Church where his daughter and the other children practice their faltering lessons on the various instruments. That music leads to "emotion" in the fourth section, where the narrator relates the substance of the novel he never wrote about a computer programmer who dies, romantically, from the strain of an adulterous affair. This unlucky bloom of the narrator's imagination deeply affects him, and it prompts the renewed vision of the fifth section, one in which the themes of Eucharist, music, adultery, and suffering coalesce to form an original metaphor of the world as Host. Like the tough wafer of the revised Communion sacrament, the world "must be chewed" to insure one's active involvement; it dare no longer simply melt in the mouth as one passively absorbs it.

"The Music School" has no plot, no narrative continuity; it borrows the format of the informal essay but is fiction. How then are the motifs organized to produce an artistic integrity? For one, at the end of the tale, the narrator suggests that a "coda" is fitting to conclude the piece, hinting at a direct musical analogy. One can observe thematic variations, contrapuntal effects, and a polyphonic-like manipulation of motifs that strengthen the parallel to musical composition. The eating motif, for example, is mentioned in the initial section in the description of the Communion wafer; it is varied and continued in the second section: the computer expert is murdered while he sits at the breakfast table. In the third section it appears briefly in the self-denial of the daughter (she doesn't ask her father for candy), and in the final section it is developed through the narrator's memory of the Lutheran Eucharist celebration, a consubstantial eating of the body of Christ, the image of which is transferred at the end to the metaphor of the world that must be chewed to be fully experienced.

Or, again, the polyphonic use of themes is illustrated in the adultery trope. The celibacy of priests and the chastity of

nuns in the initial section contrast with the brothel metaphor
of the second. Within the context of childhood innocence in the
third section, the narrator abruptly confesses his unfaithfulness;
and, in the fourth, he imagines the hero of his unwritten novel
to be dying of sexual guilt. In the last section, the reference to
the role of persisting sexuality in failed marriages restates
the trope in a discursive form. These themes are then mingled
and merged, as in a musical composition, throughout the different sections. For example, the murdered computer expert
becomes the passionate adulterous hero of the unwritten novel,
and the reported detail of the programmer's death (he dies at
the feet of his children) is transformed into the final image of the
story, when the narrator's child comes to him from her lesson,
and he writes, "her pleased smile, biting her lower lip, pierces
my heart, and I die (I think I am dying) at her feet." Or the
wafer that melts too soon serves as an analogy to explain why
the narrator never wrote his novel: "the moment in my life it
was meant to crystallize dissolved too quickly," just as it leads
him to consider the necessity of harsh experiences (the tough
wafer) for successfully encountering the unsentimental modern
world.

A magnificent scene in the final section returns the reader to
the guiding quotation and clarifies the overriding intention of
the story. As the narrator sat, the previous night, with the priest
and other friends, "a woman entered without knocking; she had
come from the lawyers, and her eyes and hair were flung wide
with suffering, as if she had come in out of a high wind. She
saw our black-garbed guest, was amazed, ashamed perhaps, and
took two backward steps. But then, in the hush, she regained
her composure and sat down among us." She is like the music
school angels who "fumble, pause, and begin again,"—and that
describes also how Updike's painfully married people carry on
in their dislocated society. They agonize, they are without
direction, but they do not give up. They experiment and practice
with the few given entities of their being, like the composer of
music and like the "author" of the story himself; for they have,
often, only the memory of grace (the recollection of the traditional Communion service), a precarious truce with the impersonal computer-culture about them, and the doubtful comfort
of their continuing erotic vitality. But they maintain their
courage and their wit; and, if they do not have the promise

any longer of achieving finesse on life's instrument, they at least create a personal meaning in the act of trying.

IV "The Rescue"

In the final section of "The Music School," Updike has his narrator say, "Each moment I live, I must think where to place my fingers, and press them down with no confidence of hearing a chord. My friends are like me. We are all pilgrims, faltering toward divorce." This elliptical combination of extremely self-conscious artistry and the recognition that failing marriages are a modern matter-of-course event seems surprisingly disjointed at first, but it is not so. Federico Fellini's famous 8½ film, for example, is a work that employs a similar strategy. It is a movie of a director trying unsuccessfully to make a movie, just as Updike's story shows an author trying to write a story he cannot; and in both instances an inhibiting marriage and adulterous relationship are a contributing cause of the failure. The rationale of the failure is patent: both the artistic effort and the marriage union require a degree of *natural* response, and the entry of hyperself-awareness is symptomatic of a loss of trust. In the artist's situation, it is a loss of trust in his creative powers; in marriage, the loss of faith in the partner.

In "The Rescue," the story immediately following "The Music School," Updike focuses on the second facet: the disintegration of confidence in one's mate and the struggle to regain it through and in spite of the curse of self-consciousness. The setting is a new one for Updike (and one that he returns to later for a crucial sexual encounter of characters in *Couples*). Caroline Harris, a New England housewife, is with her son and husband at a New Hampshire ski resort. They are accompanied by Alice Smith, their divorcée neighbor, who, Caroline suspects, is sleeping with her husband. Riding up the ski lift with Alice, with the two males in the jolting chairs ahead of them, Caroline suffers the secret anger and jealousy of her unspoken accusation. She probes, therefore, for nuances of behavior that will betray Alice but finds nothing to confirm or assuage her fears. When the two Harris males ski away without waiting for the women, Caroline and Alice continue together down the "Greased Lightning" slope that frightens Caroline, a novice skier. Midway down the hill they come upon an accident: an older woman has hurt her leg in a fall and lies in the snow with her daughter kneeling at her side. Alice and Caroline remain with the woman while the daughter goes for help. In that span of time, while they are waiting for the rescue, Caroline watches her neighbor's fussy behavior during this mild emergency and decides that her husband could not, after all, "love anyone so finicking." When the rescue party arrives, she skis off smoothly, better than ever before, to her exonerated mate.

In reality, Caroline has solved nothing; she has not proved or disproved the existence of an affair. But she has convinced herself of her husband's innocence, at least for the time being; and her conviction is more important, for the time being, than the factual truth. It is more important, in Updike's context of fragile and broken marriages, because it takes a gesture of trust to create a truthful situation. One trusts, in other words, not because the partner is necessarily trustworthy but because such an attitude is the only one that allows for a sane and reasonably civilized relationship.

But even the impulse to trust cannot be generated in the extremely self-conscious atmosphere of modern marriage, and it is appropriate that Caroline Harris overcomes her suspicions and regains trust through a situation that demands forgetfulness of self. In the unself-consciousness that a moment of kindness and concern brings, she gains an assurance, illusory though it may be, that will help her to encounter her husband and marriage—at least to a degree—naturally and non-analytically again. She is one who, faltering toward divorce (skiing dangerously down the treacherous slope), finds the proper balance at the last moment. That she glides confidently and eagerly toward her husband, her skis feeling right for the first time, implies that she has also discovered a style of life before it is too late.

The title "The Rescue" carries an ambiguous but not an ironic connotation. The central physical action of the story, the rescue of the injured woman on the mountain side, parallels Caroline's own deliverance. It is revelation via metaphor; Caroline "did not as a rule like self-pitying women, but here in this one she seemed to confront a voluntary dramatization of her own inner sprain." In watching the other, she sees herself reflected; in helping her, she begins to heal herself. There is no implication that she mends her marital situation, for her doing so might be too much to expect in the pilgrims' progress toward divorce.

But she does regain her sense of fidelity, the healthiest antidote
she could possess against her husband's suspected or actual unfaithfulness.

V *"My Lover Has Dirty Fingernails"*

"My Lover Has Dirty Fingernails" takes place in a psycho-
analyst's office in a large city (New York?) and presents a
feint-and-parry account of one session involving the doctor and
his female patient. The story works consciously with the modern
cliché of the emotional transference: the patient's falling in
love with the analyst. The woman (married but unnamed in
the story) is in the process of giving up her lover and is apparently visiting the psychiatrist to ease herself through the crisis.
As the title and the dialogue during the session reveal, her
problem is the need to fight off an acute fear of death, and her
subconsciously dictated strategy is her involvement with an
earthy man who is, for her, a counteraction to the sterile and
mortality-ridden city atmosphere.

But the emerging diagnosis is really only the superficial
content of the tale; more important is the artistic handling of
the super-aware excursion into the mind—one for which Updike
uses a neat and simple device. He has the analyst distract the
woman by objectifying the affair through the dissecting conversation and by shifting her attention subtly to himself. Most
impressively, one experiences his success through the changes
of perspective in the story. The woman's point of view appears
throughout most of the narrative; but, toward the end, it gradually becomes the doctor's. In the final paragraph, the woman
has left the office, and the doctor remains alone as the focus of
interest.

The reader is left, nonetheless, at the end of the story with
the feeling that the woman's "cure" may be worse than the
neurosis. The doctor *is* winning, as he realizes; he remains
coolly professional during his confrontation with his patient;
but what he offers her, though it may be equilibrium, is made
to seem less than the passion she is sacrificing. "At least I loved
somebody who loved me, no matter how silly you make the
reasons for it seem," she tells the analyst near the end of the
hour. When one compares her sentiment to the final scene of
the story—after the woman has gone, the psychiatrist "subsided

into the tranquil surface of the furniture"—one finds that there
may be, after all, a strange kind of affirmation in the chaotic
lives of Updike's couples. They are still struggling with identity
and love; they have not yet become part of the furniture; and,
if their adulterous affairs are attempts to know others so that
they will not know themselves too well, they escape thereby
some of the dehumanization that threatens urban man. The
psychoanalytically-induced self-knowledge is not a final answer:
it is only a diagnosis; and passion must find a new mode of
expression that provides both self-forgetfulness and legitimate
freedom. Updike's people have not found that mode, but neither
has contemporary American society.

VI   *Other Marriage Tales: Introspection, Passion, and Separation*

The other six marriage stories compose variations on the same
introspection-passion-separation theme. In "Avec la Bébé-sitter,"
an American family moves suddenly from Boston to the French
Riviera to escape the husband's entanglement in an affair. On
the sensual Mediterranean, where one would expect, perhaps,
a seductive French governess who corrupts the marriage of innocent Americans, one finds instead a rather dowdy middle-aged
widow who tries to help the family regain its composure. As
baby sitter, she exposes the family's childishness: the husband
and wife, instead of solving their marital problems, allow themselves to be taken care of—and this strange ménage is a symptom
of a destructive liaison rather than a cure for it.

The epistolary "Four Sides of One Story," a quasi-moderniza-
tion of the Tristan and Iseult legend, exists, like *The Centaur*,
in a tension between the accepted unbelievability of folklore
and the more insistent realism of modern fiction. But, where
The Centaur takes advantage of the incongruity by making
ancient myth and contemporary narrative elucidate each other,
"Four Sides of One Story" offers no real justification for the
baggage of the legend. Using it is merely a clever gimmick,
although the story, as is always the case with Updike, contains
moments of authentic feeling. The characterization is, however,
too radically limited by what one knows of the folklore personae,
and Updike does not manage to make his characters either
figures of independent substance or complements to the legendary ones.

"Leaves," which is more of a prose-poem than conventional fiction, is a five-page, present-tense confession of a man who is learning to face himself again in the shambles of a recent divorce and—as much as one can tell—an attempted reconciliation. Self-exiled for an emotional cure in a isolated forest cottage, he orders his shattered world dualistically, through the purity of nature contrasted with his sense of guilt. In this secular reconciliation process, the imagination replaces faith; and natural innocence offers its own measure of grace.

"The Stare" and "The Morning" are parallel narratives. In the first, the speaker returns to Manhattan to search for his former lover at their old haunts. He has ended the affair that had had both their households in turmoil; now, months later, he hopes to find her again. The story is built on the counteraction between repetitive image and sustained anticipation. His lover's curious stare, the most striking feature she possesses, is the image he needs to re-encounter; and Updike always balances the man's recollection of that glance with his frustration at missing it now in his persistent New York search. Duped by some trait he had thought was hers alone, he follows look-alikes of his mistress; but he always comes close only to see not her stare but the unfamiliar face of an utter stranger. In this story the basic thematic sequence (introspection-passion-separation) is reversed and becomes separation-passion-introspection. The isolation from the lover induces new desire, but it leads not to fulfillment—only to pathetic self-confrontation.

"Love begins in earnest when we love what is limited," is the theme of "The Morning," and the text is given elaborate substance by an artistic concentration on color. Color not only forms moods here but also creates actual states of being in the sole "premarital" story of the collection. The protagonist (who reminds one of Dostoevski's Underground Man) is a young student—"of what, he had forgotten"—in the big city who has just been deserted by his lover, a nurse, because he will not marry her. The girl has left him, and he has only the sensuous-sensual memories; but she has left him so recently that memory is still part reflex, and he lives in half-anticipation of her return. The stages of his desire for her assume various colors: the white of her uniform connotes a professional purity that excites him; the blue, green, and brown of her off-duty clothes (some still in his closet) represent the normal world outside that she channeled to him;

and the tan, blonde, and pink of her nakedness hold the remem-
bered adventure and intimacy of their love.

Because the nurse is the center of his existence, her absence
establishes the sense of the void which the reader feels along
with the grieving student. The point of view never leaves the
student's mind or the confines of the shabby apartment. This
use of a restricted center of consciousness perspective reveals
how utterly vacuous the student's daily life without his lover
must be. The story reinforces its emotional effect through two
expanded puns. The one is the concept of the nurse. "My nurse,"
the young man calls her; and, while he means it affectionately,
it also hints at the psychological sickness he endures: he needs
her as a substitute for the city outside. She has been the mediator
and buffer between the world and him; and, in relating to her,
he finds his surrogate and fulfillment for all responsibilities and
desires. Because the girl is healthier than he is, she leaves him;
and the consequence informs the story's title, "The Morning."
The morning, that time of day when the nurse comes to him
to minister to him, is now "the mourning"; for she has
gone, and he is in fresh sorrow, still disbelieving his loss and only
beginning to absorb its magnitude. Passion-separation-introspec-
tion is the sequence in this story, but their effect on the protagonist is nearly simultaneous.

The remaining marriage story, "Harv Is Plowing Now," has
a partial Olinger setting and unites the now-dominant marital
theme with the childhood reminiscence. The story moves through
fictive personal recollection into universal history: the man who
has grown up on the Pennsylvania farm and suffered through—
still suffers—the effects of an affair sees his life stratified like
the exposed layers of an archeological find. At the bottom is
the mythic substance of the collective unconscious, compressed
in the childhood memory of Harv, the neighboring farmer,
plowing his field in the recurrent spring ritual of fertility and
rebirth. At the top are the myriad hours and days of mechanical
time passing; and, in the middle, providing its own kind of
existence, is the experience of the affair, past and yet present.

Updike makes the analogy with archeological exploration (actually a multi-directed metaphor) work by playing with motif-
phrases as in "The Music School." The great Noachic flood and
the "inundation" of the love affair, the excavation of Ur and
Harv's plowing, the digging at the desert find and the probing

into the old affair on a bonfire-lit beach at night—these, grasped in configurational form, provide the sense of precariousness of one's sojourn in time and space but also one's fundamental security. Passion has failed, but the natural rites and one's personal survival are intact. The farmer plows, the archeologist digs, the artist probes the memory—and all do so to effect some sort of resurrection. The artist recovers an incident from his personal past (an operation not nearly as trivial as it seems) and gives it a permanent place by locating it not in literal space-time but in metaphor.

History and fact, in other words, must deal with the finite and with the temporary, like the love affair that forms the content of the story; but the fictive transformation brings about something lasting. What matters to the self-conscious artist is not that the event literally took place but that he can use it as a device for structuring his universe. The experience of the affair may be like an artifact (as Updike renders it in this tale) to be carefully exhumed from the memory and the unconscious, but the story *about* the experience also possesses its archeological parallel. Fiction is the artifact that remains fiction until somewhere and sometime the reader strikes the solid truth of metaphoric recognition and uncovers a relationship to himself that helps to order his being.

VII   *People from the Family Album*

The other nine stories in *The Music School* collection fit no particular pattern. Taken together, they give one the sensation of paging through an old photo album—a pastime Updike is said to enjoy—and stopping here and there to study striking or eccentric characters. Three of the stories return, in degrees, to the old Olinger setting. "In Football Season," the first narrative of the book, has echoes of the high school scenes in *The Centaur* and is a sharply evocative mood story. "The Family Meadow," in contrast, is mellow, like the fading pictures in the album. It describes a family reunion in a rural enclave of New Jersey (Olinger relatives are in attendance), and the mellowness grows against the awareness of accelerating change. Both the promise and the threat of the future pervade the reunion. The provocative teenaged Cousin Karin, half-Italian, in her tight, white Levis embodies the obliteration of the old family lines and the exciting new shapes that appear. The new houses of the building project on the fringes of the meadow, with their "bastard design," hold mainly the threat not of heterogeneity but of mass-produced uniformity like that depicted in *The Poorhouse Fair*.

The conflict in "The Family Meadow" is basically between nature and civilization; but, in the final story, "The Hermit," Updike purifies and climaxes that antagonism. Stanley, a middle-aged school janitor and part-time laborer for his contractor brother, chooses to withdraw from the village to live in the ruins of an old farmhouse surrounded by fields now reclaimed by the forest. His retreat into nature is also a mystical growth, but it seems to his convention-bound relatives and friends that he is degenerating from eccentricity into sheer craziness. A bit like Ike McCaslin in Faulkner's *The Bear*, Stanley must cast off the extraneous accumulations of society to experience nature totally—to become, as he feels it, "a thoroughly silver man." But his ritual purification is much more radical than Ike's: Stanley smashes his mirror, rejects visitors, stops reading, and bathes daily in his tiny, cold stream. His freedom at last undoes him when, returning naked from his bath one day, he surprises an eavesdropper, a young boy and potential disciple; and he chases the terrified youngster through the woods to reassure him, not to assault or punish him. Three days later he is taken away forcibly as a menace to society, for his intent was never understood.

This ending may seem like a surprising last word from Updike, the advocate of enduring the middle-class life of quiet frustration, until one understands that eccentricity is a kind of vocation. It dawns on Stanley that to be a hermit is his calling; it is what he has been instinctively preparing himself for. Indeed, in *The Music School* other eccentrics figure in other tales; and the Indian (in the second story entitled "The Indian") provides a contrast to Stanley the hermit's egression. The Indian has moved out of nature into the New England town of Tarbox; he inhabits the village, jobless and yet proprietary, an enigmatic degeneration of his forebears but a silent judge of the moral heritage and present manners of the town. His vocation is his otherness.

The eccentric in "A Madman," the fourth story in *The Music School*, is Mr. Robinson, the self-appointed guide to a young American, who is newly arrived in Oxford to study English literature, and to his pregnant wife. Mr. Robinson, a humanist antique, is a walking and endlessly talking repository of poetry and impractical knowledge who attaches himself to the innocent Americans; rather than helping them find the flat they need, he conducts them (to their confusion and exasperation) through the cultural riches of the old university town. The tour is not just a matter of poor timing: the old man is obsolete even in Oxford, a slightly dotty relic of learning in a world that, perhaps to its misfortune, has passed him by.

"At a Bar in Charlotte Amalie" has an extensive catalogue of eccentrics. The Bahama tourist setting allows for the gathering of strange characters in the bar. A scenic story with a deceptive forward movement, everything in it—language, gesture, description—is purposeful innuendo, to express the subtlety of sexual maneuvering among strangers. When at least two liaisons develop by the end, one recognizes that they have been in the making all along. The homosexual from Queens, although not quite the protagonist, is the focal point, the catalyst of the action, and the grotesque mediator between the straight world and a sub-world that exists as much in a collective unconscious as it does in the physical locale of the bar. This story uses the psychic stuff of Freud, Jung, and Sacher-Masoch; people wear their favorite aberrations like the latest fashion. That they are portrayed not as freaks but as credible personalities makes their behavior all the more disturbing. They are like Updike's quiet, middle-class neurotics suddenly put on Expressionistic display; their condition is rendered brutally public, so that they appear both pathetic and frightening.

"The Christian Roommates," Updike's only Harvard story to date, has Hub Palamountain, a young skeptic from Oregon, as its eccentric. He is the despair of Orson Ziegler, his proper South Dakota roommate; for Hub's unorthodox views and practices nearly unbalance Orson during their nerve-wracking freshman year in Cambridge. The irony of the tale is in the unusual opportunity that Hub presents to Orson: Hub could *be* his roommate's Harvard education, but Orson has already planned his life so meticulously and staidly that he never even sees the possibility; therefore, he receives only training and not a genuine education there. In this story the maverick has more humanity and compassion than the conventional pillar of the community. Hub is a wise fool, one who muddles through the irrationality of the age because he himself is comfortably balmy and not a neurotic struggling to locate some normalcy in himself or his surroundings.

It seems, at first, that "The Dark" concerns an insomniac fighting a case of nerves as he tries to find sleep. One then discovers that he is incurably ill (probably of lung cancer, for it is obliquely described) and that his sleeplessness, naturally enough, arises from a fear of death. The title refers to the agonizing loneliness of his present situation and also to the impending end of life, including his unanswered questions about immortality. His sleep at last is also a prefiguring of death: to "slip, blissfully, into oblivion" is an image for the nightly rest he seeks and for the death he anticipates.

VIII *Through the Mirror*

Updike prefaces *The Music School* with lines from Wallace Stevens' poem, "To the One of Fictive Music." With an emphasis on the intricate interrelationships of nature, art, and love, the selection (like much of Stevens' verse) verbalizes a poetic entelechy. The subject-object dichotomy of one's creatureliness can be resolved in the act of love when that experience is articulated in a poetic celebration of it. In loving, one overcomes self-consciousness; but, in the poetic shaping of the experience, one gains a measure of esthetic distance without dissolving the experience itself. If it is true, as Sartre has said, that the ultimate evil lies in making abstractions out of concrete things, then Updike must be praised for trying the opposite. In naming and describing the adultery, the betrayal, the necessary separation, he tames the abstraction and makes it less terrible, makes it what it is in individual terms, and allows one to deal with it individually.

Updike's total vision seems less entelechial than Stevens' and more eschatological. One strives to see through the mirror to the Other. To say this is not just to substitute a theological concept for a philosophical one. The actualizing moment of entelechy is not the same as eschatological faith, and Updike's fiction drives distinctly toward the latter. Since this book is not the place to discuss Updike's theological vision, suffice it to say that he has one; and even in *The Music School,* when his people are touching uncertain chords, they are playing a composition that has already been written. A faith in divinity lingers even in the efforts of self-consciously secular man.

CHAPTER *8*

Couples:
Tristan and Don Juan in Tarbox

Their universe did not deserve their vows.
—from "Room 28"

I   *The Culmination of Secular Baroque*

C OUPLES seems to be Updike's answer to the critics who have
frequently wondered publicly when he would write a "big"
novel. In terms of concept and physical format, at least, it is
an ambitious work (over 450 pages) that focuses on ten married
pairs living in Tarbox, Massachusetts. Yet it was not, on the
whole, received positively by the book reviewers.¹ Its sexual
attitudes and expressions were called sophomoric; its images
overblown, its dialogue overwritten; its characters dull and
virtually indistinguishable; its action erratic and unfulfilled.

Nevertheless, this novel is the third sensation that Updike
has created, after *Rabbit, Run* and *The Centaur*. The explicit
yet poetically written sex scenes and the liberal use of formerly
taboo language caused *Couples* to be treated as both a reflection and a generator of the post-censorship literary atmosphere.
It remained on the best-seller lists for a good half-year
following its early 1968 publication. As Updike himself laconically explained his purpose in a news magazine interview, "There's
a lot of dry talk around about love and sex being somehow the
new ground of our morality. . . . I thought I should describe the
ground and ask, is it entirely to be wished for?"² As frequently
happens, the furor accompanying the depiction of sexual amoral-
ity increased the difficulty of judging the novel's artistic quality.
Most of the reviews appeared to be impulsive reactions to the
subject matter rather than measured assessments.

The novel can also be understood in terms of what is called

130

in the introduction to this book Updike's "secular baroque" because of its elaborate complexity and its attention to voluptuous incidents that create large and symmetrical patterns. Even the adultery motif shares in the baroque form; for a hazardous order inhabits these vital but always potentially chaotic relationships; and, if one component fails, the whole configuration disintegrates. It is *secular* baroque because its emphasis is on the modern concept of the relativity of the universe, not the precise divine order of the eighteenth century. The ten couples constitute a substitute church, at least in the fancy of some of them; but they also find secular absolutes to replace religion: scientific inquiry, vocation, psychoanalysis, and of course, the ritual-mystique of sex. Finally, the novel is secular baroque in its undeniably static quality. One has the curious sense of experiencing topographical time in *Couples*, something like viewing the figures on the gently domed ceiling of a baroque church: everything is immediately *there;* little progression occurs; and divisions of past, present, and future are replaced by the relative proximity of scenes and events to the centers of action. The intricate patterning of the whole substitutes, therefore, for a strong emphasis on sequentiality. The idea of secular baroque is important to an understanding of *Couples* because Updike fashions a number of devices that derive from a religious understanding of existence but deny finally traditional religiosity in favor of a modern pattern. The simultaneousness of temporality already mentioned, for example, is an aspect of this novel that questions the Western Christian understanding of time and that suggests, instead, not the older cyclical repetition of existence but something like the Einsteinian bent space theory. Updike's fascination with time moves beyond his treatment of it in *The Centaur* and reaches a new sophistication in *Couples*.

Just as important, the uniformity of characters that some critics have complained about is not the result of careless writing but the result of the intentional creation of a composite protagonist that has as its model not the individualism of Romanticism or of the Victorian era but the desired organic unity of the modern corporation or of other such megastructures. *Couples* expands beyond these metaphors of corporate unity into an elaboration of a religiously infused symbol and myth-legend. The symbol centers on the function of the adulterous group as a quasi-church, while the myth-legend has two poles: the embodiment of the Tristan and Don Juan archetypes in the characters, imagery, and action. These four devices—the new treatment of time, the composite protagonist, the group symbolized as quasi-church, the two archetypes—have the total effect of gradually translating the absolutist religious orientation into a contemporary relativist viewpoint.

Updike's fictitious Tarbox is a small town in Plymouth County, Massachusetts, almost on the Atlantic Ocean and twenty-two miles southeast of Boston. Nine of the ten couples in the story already inhabit Tarbox at the start of the novel; they are middle-class to upper-middle-class members of the community; they are, on the average, in their mid-thirties; and most of them have children. Piet Hanema, who comes closest to being an individual protagonist, is a thirty-five-year-old building contractor of Dutch descent; he and his wife Angela have two small daughters. Piet is having an affair early in the novel with Georgene Thorne, whose husband Freddy is a dentist in Tarbox and who is also a kind of Lord of Misrule at parties. Piet's partner in the construction business is Matt Gallagher, a puritanical Catholic whose wife Terry has an affair with her pottery teacher, an older man who is not part of the group. Piet also sleeps eventually with Bea Guerin, whose husband Roger is independently wealthy and doesn't need to work. Two other sets of couple have interrelationships of various sorts. Of these, Frank and Janet Appleby and Harold and Marcia Smith (the other couples call the four the Applesmiths) trade spouses for a time, while the Jewish pair Ben and Irene Saltz and airline pilot Eddie Constantine and his wife Carol ("the Saltines"—Piet also sleeps with Carol) have a liaison that includes homosexual impulses. A bit on the fringes of this group are a ninth couple: the Korean nuclear physicist John Ong and his American wife Bernadette.

Into this group come a tenth couple from Cambridge, research biologist Ken Whitman and his pregnant wife Foxy. The Whitmans hire Piet to renovate the house they have bought close to Tarbox Bay, and Piet's frequent presence at the house leads to an affair with Foxy. He sleeps with her during the months of her pregnancy (and gradually gives up Georgene) and continues to do so soon after the baby is born. Foxy becomes pregnant again, this time by Piet; and, when it becomes apparent

that something must be done, they arrange through Freddy
Thorne to visit a Boston abortionist. Freddy's price, before the
abortion takes place, is a night with Angela Hanema. Although
Angela does not understand the situation, she (quite incredibly)
agrees to sleep with Freddy; and they spend a night together
at a ski resort. Freddy becomes impotent and cannot make love
with her, but the terms of the bargain have been fulfilled, so he
takes Foxy and Piet to Boston. The abortion is successful, and
no one is the wiser until some time later Georgene, in a fit of
jealousy, tells Ken Whitman of the affair and the abortion. Ken
and Foxy separate, and Foxy goes to the Virgin Islands. Angela
and Piet also separate, and eventually both couples are divorced.
Piet sells his share in the construction business to his partner,
marries Foxy at last, and the two move to Lexington, where
Piet becomes a building inspector.

Such a sketch by no means conveys the power of the novel
or even the total scope of the action, merely its skeletal structure.
For instance, the second chapter, "Applesmiths and Other
Games," does not focus on Piet and Foxy at all but on the double
affair among the Smiths and Applebys. Nor does this summary
indicate the importance of the many parties among the couples,
that of the family scenes involving children, that of the destruction of the Tarbox Congregational Church by fire, or that of
the fine stream-of-consciousness passages that fill in background
action. An analysis of the four devices listed earlier will convey
further a sense of the richness of *Couples*.

II *The Topography of Time*

Although the architecture of temporality is not as immediately
evident in *Couples* as in *The Centaur*, it is just as fundamental
to the later novel. *Couples is* a static novel, yet Updike has aligned
this narrative more directly to a historical epoch than any of
his other fiction except *Rabbit Redux*. Much of the action occurs
in 1963, during the final year of the John F. Kennedy presidency;
and the action is, in fact, dramatically punctured by the news of
his assassination. References are made also to Kennedy and the
Cuban missile crisis, to Kennedy and the steel industry, to U
Thant and Tschombe in the Congo, to tensions between Arabs
and Israelis, and to Charles De Gaulle, Marina Oswald, and Ho
Chi Minh—all events and names that appear in texts about mod-

ern national and international history. But Updike provides in addition a sense of cyclical time by celebrating the passing and return of the seasons, by the pattern of Foxy's two pregnancies, and by the final sentence of the book: "The Hanemas live in Lexington, where, gradually, among people like themselves, they have been accepted, as another couple."

All these dimensions of time are put into a mythological focus at the end of the fourth chapter by the declaration of Freddy Thorne (who is in bed with Angela) that this is "one of those dark ages that visits mankind between millennia, between the death and rebirth of gods, when there is nothing to steer by but sex and stoicism and the stars." This statement carries some of the feeling of a third kind of time, a sort of suspension that pervades *Couples*. It is the feeling of traveling in a vast universe without actually moving anywhere, a universe in which history is being made that the individual inhabitants do not mold and that has no apparent meaning for them.

Couples has a number of narrative climaxes, but the action (as in *The Music School* stories), because of Updike's peculiar use of time, abandons the traditional crescendo pattern of fiction. That pattern demands linearity ("linearity" is in this context a spatial metaphor for a temporal concept), a movement from one moment to another to create suspense, anticipation, and fulfillment. Linearity is basic to the Christian sense of time, while the traditional opposite of linearity is circularity, as in Stoicism and certain pessimistic Medieval doctrines and Eastern philosophies. All are imaged, for example, in fortune's wheel: life's significant events repeat themselves in cyclical fashion. *Couples* projects a time beyond the linear and cyclical. The counterpart to the void that one feels in the novel is simultaneousness, in which many things happen at once and everything is now. This simultaneousness that fills the book is, of course, a mood rather than a physical fact; but, since Updike's people (and the reader) feel it so intensely, it is as important as the physical fact. To produce such simultaneousness, Updike uses memory and association effectively. For instance, the squeaking noise that the children's pet hamster makes on his exercise wheel—*eek eeik*—reminds Piet of the native Dutch that his parents spoke; thereby, three generations are instantaneously joined. Dreams also (mostly Piet's) distort conventional time and create the illusion of omnipresence.

An atmosphere of fulfillment, of *telos*, that pervades the novel characterizes yet another kind of temporality. It is not apocalyptic, not the terrible exhilaration of an age ending in chaos (unlike the tone of many another contemporary novel), and not utopian, as if a new, perfect age were arriving. It is a distinct recognition of *having* arrived in "the post-pill paradise" and of discovering that this age is as frustrating and chaotic as any other. But the discovery is not all negative. For example, Freddy Thorne, charmed by vice, learns with some wonder that he and his friends are "all put here to *humanize* each other"; and this responsibility becomes a new challenge to the Tarbox mentality. The society that confronts itself in ripeness, in a full sensuality of experience, becomes jaded by mere sensation and seeks a deeper intrinsic meaning. To return to the analogy from architecture, when the Gothic and Renaissance aspiration "upward" (the movement toward an ideal future and toward transcendence) is arrested and the reaching spires are rounded and internalized into baroque domes, the complex richness of the present replaces both the veneration of the past and the stylized striving toward the future; and then immanence and self-realization become central.

III   *The Composite Protagonist*

A certain sameness marks the Tarbox pairs: they are all in their thirties, they all endure the combined banes and blessings of suburbia, they share an intellectual depth that is a good degree greater than the storied adult-American television mentality and they are all affected by the hyper-sexuality of the group. They tend to sound alike in their conversations, and they are also described through an imagery that does not dramatically individualize them. Nevertheless, such characterization does not reveal poor craftsmanship; for, since the couples are presented as an intimate group, it is entirely credible to make them more homogeneous than the aggregate of personae in most other novels. One sees Updike's couples as strongly influenced by each other; but, beyond this interaction, Updike seems more concerned about interrelationships than about individuals. *Couples* is a novel about group dynamics rather than about the fortunes of a hero. It is a configurative novel in which the parts of individual personalities are joined to form a composite, a group personality.

The complexity and even symmetry of the relationships in *Couples* show the "baroque" bias in Updike's characterization. It is quite ironic that the disorder of adultery should be expressed in such precise balances and nuances of sexual activity, but that is how the novel interprets life. Modes of behavior with the least societal approval evolve a very stringent sort of order. Thus Piet and Georgene as lovers, and later Piet and Foxy, develop elaborate rituals of courtesy in this most intimate of relationships; and such orderliness extends to broader group interactions. The spouse-swapping between the Smiths and Applebys proceeds, in spite of the underlying bitchery, with great tact; and the confrontation between the Hanemas and Whitmans, after the affair is exposed, is diplomatic and formally correct. More interesting still, from an "architecture of fiction" perspective, is the elaborate pattern of extramarital liaisons in *Couples*: Piet, married to Angela, sleeps with Georgene (who is married to Freddy) but leaves her for Foxy (married to Ken); Freddy, who arranges the abortion for Foxy, reveals the affair to jealous Georgene, who betrays Piet and Foxy to Ken and brings about two divorces. (In the meanwhile, Freddy has also slept with Angela as his price for arranging the abortion.) All of the arrangements are precariously exact, in other words; and if one part goes awry the whole design collapses. This pattern creates the remarkable suspense that fills a static novel; one awaits the false move that will initiate the fall.

The symmetry appears in the balancing of the Applesmiths' double affair with the combinations of the Saltines, in the fact that Piet beds down with exactly five of the ten wives, and in the contrast of Freddy's impotent lust with Piet's guilty fornication. Social sex assumes an esthetic integrity through the fullness of Updike's style. Rather negatively, on the other hand, he has illustrated a sociological verity that citizens of the late twentieth century are reluctantly accepting: that the accent on humans living together—on the corporate, organic aspect of life—is at least as important as the old mythically reinforced concept of unfettered individuality. The composite protagonist of *Couples* represents an awareness of the changing emphasis in societal forms and attempts to use the chemistry of group interaction more than individual behavior as a metaphor of human nature and society at large.

IV *The Substitute Church*

The truth is also that these people do not live well together, and one wonders why they continue to seek one another's company. One reason stressed by the dialogue and imagery is that they function, in this complex secular era, as a substitute church. The implication is not, however, that Updike is suggesting a return to the "real" church as a panacea for social and personal ills; but, he is obviously illustrating a belief that man without God needs some sort of surrogate, and, perhaps, that a destructive fellowship is better than none at all. However that may be, the novel frequently borrows the image of the church to clarify the characters' motives and actions. For example, Angela, when discussing with her husband the jaded condition of the group, cites Freddy's analysis: "He thinks we're a circle. A magic circle of heads to keep the night out. He told me he gets frightened if he doesn't see us over a weekend. He thinks we've made a church of each other."

More convincing than such overt declarations are the couples' actions that become substitute ritual and sacramental behavior. Some of these are conscious travesties, such as the morbid moment at the dinner party following President Kennedy's assassination, when Freddy, slicing ham, says, "Take, eat. . . . This is his body, given for thee." The scene would be blasphemous if a situation sensitive to blasphemy still existed; but, as it is used in the novel, the crude Eucharistic joke masks the need of the couples for fellowship and communion at a time of grief and despair. A dinner party on the night of Kennedy's death is not merely a thoughtless vulgarity but also the fumbling attempt of spiritually helpless people to ease their desolation. Food, drink, and sexual excitement are ingredients in the ritual that induces intimacy; and intimacy is necessary to counteract the personal dislocation caused by the shock of the assassination.

The conflagration of the church at the end of the novel must also be understood in the light of its ironic ritualistic import. Many reviews of *Couples* chided Updike for the blatant symbolism of the fire: the burning edifice signifying the end of the church as an institution, destroyed by the hot passion of sex. Such an interpretation is far too simplistic. The destruction of the church, itself a crucial ritual moment, is the one event in the novel that brings the townspeople together in an act of com-

mon interest; it is an ironic moment because they are united by
destruction rather than by creation.[3]

V   *Tristan and Don Juan*

If Freddy Thorne is a perverse priest who guides his little
congregation in the celebration of sensuality, he and his "church"
are still not necessarily dedicated to evil. Rather, the ecclesiastical
analogy seems to argue either that secular man needs to assert
and reinforce his identity through sacred ceremony or that the
believer must learn to accommodate the reality of the body in
his faith. Updike explores both of these possibilities in *Couples*
by offering suggestions of the Tristan and Don Juan legends.
Updike had used the Tristan legend in a modern setting in "Four
Sides of One Story" in *The Music School* collection. Before the
appearance of that tale, he had exhibited his interest in the
Tristan and Don Juan types through his *New Yorker* review of
Denis de Rougemont's *Love in the Western World* and *Love
Declared*.[4] In this review, he used the Swiss critic's works as a
basis for declaring his own views about *Eros*, marriage, the death
wish, and the search for meaning.

It is quite obvious that *Couples* builds thoroughly and
extensively on Updike's continuing concern—although not
always agreement—with de Rougemont's treatment of the passion myths. In his review, Updike asserts with de Rougemont
that Tristan and Don Juan typify even in the twentieth century
contrasting attitudes toward passion and marriage. In *Couples*,
Piet is sometimes a Tristan, sometimes a Don Juan, and sometimes
both at the same time; and the other characters supplement the
mythic structure. This double archetypal pattern proceeds
through three stages: first, the identification of the characters
of the novel with their mythic types; second, the description of
the meaning inherent in the narrative-myth combination; and
third, the clarification of a new secular vision that the novel
projects through the myth.

In the association of narrative and mythic characters, Angela
plays the most apparent contrast to Piet as Tristan. She is both
Iseult the Fair and Iseult of the White Hand; for her whiteness,
her temperamental blend of passion and aloofness, and the
otherworldly echo of her name all suggest her two roles. According to the legend, of course, Angela should be Piet's mistress

instead of his wife; but Updike changes some angles of the tale. Foxy also has the roles of the two Iseults: she is described in terms of whiteness (her name is "Whitman"; her clothing and surroundings are often depicted through white imagery) and in terms of the combination of passion and unavailability.

In his Tristan role, Piet seeks the ideal woman who will assuage his fear of death and his longing for the infinite; as Don Juan, he attempts to conquer many women in order to outdo death in a frenzy of virility and to force the secret of infinity hidden in *Eros*. In Updike's review of the de Rougemont books, he states that "Don Juan loves Woman under the guise of many women, exhaustingly";[5] and Foxy writes a similar thought to Piet from her refuge in the Caribbean: "When you desire to be the world's husband, what right do I have to make you my own?" Piet does in fact sleep with three other wives, besides Angela and Foxy; and Angela's comment (to Freddy) that "Piet spends all his energy defying death" reveals the desperate impulse behind much of his lust. Other characters reinforce Piet's Don Juan status: Eddie Constantine with his many women in Puerto Rico is one; and Freddy Thorne, another, at least articulates a Don Juan philosophy even though he does not translate it into action. The interchangeability of persons slides easily into postures of promiscuity in the Don Juan framework; the couples as composite protagonist try to wrench a meaning out of life through indiscriminate sex.

These correspondences between personae in the novel and their archetypes have important ramifications. In his review of de Rougemont, Updike elaborates on some ancient Gnostic elements that the Swiss writer sees surviving in the Tristan legend and in the Courtly Love tradition: imagery of light and darkness, a double narcissism, the Maria Sophia concept, and the search for self-identity through passion. In *Couples*, these same elements appear with striking clarity. The light-dark imagery, signifying spiritual goodness versus carnal evil in the Gnostic and Manichean traditions, is used for somewhat different ends by Updike. His characters in passionate moments together are often immersed in bright light, but their moments of loneliness and fear of death are masked by darkness. All of Piet's women are variations of the Gnostic Maria Sophia, the Mother of Christ who merges with the eternal feminine and then, in the Medieval Courtly Love tradition (according to de Rougemont), becomes the subject of erotic reverence. Angela and Foxy seem to Piet to be filled with such ethereal wisdom; his relationship to them brings him close to this mysterious power that is a further defense against death.

The double narcissism that de Rougemont seeks to expose in Tristan and Iseult as the fallacious basis of love also affects Updike's characters. Piet is a modern Courtly Lover and a "secret dandy." The couples play at illicit sex because they have made the egotistical thrill of being desired a goal in itself and do not grasp the foundation of a sound marital union. For example, after the affair between Piet and Foxy is exposed and Piet is left alone, "what he felt, remembering Foxy, was a nostalgia for adultery itself—its adventure, the acrobatics its deceptions demand, the tension of its hidden strings, the new landscapes it makes us master."

Freddy Thorne best illustrates, however, the absurdity of narcissism in *Eros*. After he finally manages to bed down with Angela (his "ideal lover"), he becomes impotent and cannot perform; but, when she falls asleep beside him, he masturbates. The unshared idea of passion is more exciting to him than a shared love relationship. Such narcissism leads in turn to the sensation of self-identity located in *Eros*. In the de Rougemont review, Updike describes it thus: "a man in love, confronting his beloved, seems to be in the presence of *his own spirit*, his self translated into another mode of being, a Form of Light greeting him at the gate of salvation."[6] Piet has this sensation with Georgene, Angela, Foxy, and Bea Guerin. He *needs* women in order to effect this mystical transformation into his true self, but it remains an essentially selfish act—as in fact many mystical efforts are.

The Don Juan model prompts similar interpretation. Updike works with concepts such as the attempted violation of life's secrets through passion, the obsession with quantity (the *number* of women seduced) instead of Tristan's economy (passionate concentration on one woman), the need for variety that degenerates into sadism to avoid boredom, and the inevitable change of the combination of *Eros* and goodness into that of *Eros* and evil. These concepts become clear in the third stage, the new secular vision that *Couples* advances through the myths. Part of this vision is the realization of a vital connection between passion and death. Tristan seeks to avoid death by losing himself in the intense love of an idealized woman, while Don Juan tries to surpass death by the seduction of many women. However, Tristan's flight from authentic relationships exposes his secret death wish, and Don Juan's exhausting compulsion in itself is fatal. Although Piet is a more convincing Tristan than a Don Juan, he does embody both of these attitudes toward passion and death, and he also reveals in the process that *Couples* stresses death as much as sex. The novel is, if anything, death-obsessed; and the sexuality that the reviewers sensationalized becomes relevant only in conjunction with death. Scene after scene emphasizes the connection of sex and death, but it is most succinctly and vulgarly metaphorized by Freddy's comment that "death is being screwed by God. It'll be delicious."

A second part of the new secular vision of *Couples*, one that follows the knowledge that participation in *Eros* only intensifies the awareness of death, is the intimation that substitutes for the Christian Incarnation persist even where the Incarnation itself is ignored. According to the traditional doctrine of the church, a basic relationship exists between love and death; God's love was demonstrated in the Incarnation of Christ, and through his sacrificial death the curse of death upon man was removed. This was *Agape*-love, a self-giving power quite different from the narcissistic passion called *Eros*. Updike remarks, summarizing de Rougemont, that "Gnosticism is an attempt to make the 'transition from Eros to the Spirit' without passing through the paradox of the Incarnation," and he may purposely be sending his Tarbox characters along the same path.[7] Since most of his people do not accept the old Christian Incarnation way but persist in a Gnostic-tinged effort toward reconciliation, they need a surrogate for the Incarnation—and they find it, of course, in sex. Toward the end of the novel, following a lyrical-philosophical description of oral sex shared by Piet and Foxy (who have now separated from their spouses), Updike writes: "Thus on the Sunday morning, beneath the hanging clangor of bells." In this passage, the physical union instead of the spiritual service on a Sunday morning, the "eating" of each other instead of the Communion wafer, and the substitution of the lovers' bodies for the body of Christ prompt the recognition that at least two of the Tarbox group are attempting an erotic embody-ment with religious overtones that is intended as a substitute for the old incarnational theology.

A third part of the new secular vision is a demythologizing process that destroys the power of the Tristan and Don Juan complexes to create a new kind of love that is more mature, permanent, and realistic. It is imaged in the marathon three-day love-making between Piet and Foxy. During that weekend they travel *through* passion and emerged purged, one feels, on the far side of promiscuity and selfish love. But the question is, what do they become? Updike implies at the close of his de Rougemont review that a myth is no longer necessary to express the contemporary situation: "Might it not simply be that sex has become involved in the Promethean protest forced upon Man by his paradoxical position in the Universe as a self-conscious animal? Our fundamental anxiety is that we do not exist—or will cease to exist. Only in being loved do we find external corroboration of the supremely high valuation each ego secretly assigns itself. This exalted arena, then, is above all others the one where men and women will insist upon their freedom to choose—to choose that other being in whose existence their own existence is confirmed and amplified."[8]

One might ask whether it is indeed true that myths are no longer necessary, whether modern man's problems of loving are not caused in part by the absence of *viable* myths of love—which is to say deeply felt beliefs about love and models for authentic loving. In any case, contemporary civilization has no archetype for the man who asserts his identity by choosing to share himself with another person (Christ is not that archetype, for he lacks the sexual dimension); therefore, a novel such as *Couples* fills an important cultural role. It suggests some possibilities for filling the void left by demythologizing and secularization—or, at the very least, it shows convincingly that the void must be filled.

CHAPTER 9

Bech: A Book:
The Protestant as Jew

See, now, the libidinous flare,
spinning on its stick in vain resistance
to the upright ego and mortality's gravity:
behold, above, the sudden bloom,
turquoise, each tip a comet,
of pride—followed, after an empty bang,
by an ebbing amber galaxy, despair.
                              —from "Fireworks"

I *The Altered Ego*

BECH: A BOOK, published in 1970, is a collection of seven stories with the same protagonist: the middle-aged Jewish novelist Henry Bech. All but two of the stories first appeared in *The New Yorker* (the exceptions are "Bech Panics" and "Bech Enters Heaven"); and one, "The Bulgarian Poetess," had appeared earlier in *The Music School*. The collection is sufficiently unified that one can read it as a loosely organized novel, with the stories representing a succession of chapters treating various episodes in the hero's life. The suggestion of a casual novel format is strengthened by a consistency of characters and actions, and by a similarity of mood and imagery in all of the tales. The details of the individual stories complement each other, and although one finds no progression of narrative as such throughout the book, the seven stories do give a fairly thorough portrait of the main character.

The book also utilizes a secondary fiction, that Bech is an actual historical person, a contemporary author whom Updike knows and is writing about. Thus Bech's own Foreword, giving his skeptical blessing to the venture, introduces the book. Two appendices also appear: the first contains excerpts from Bech's "unpublished Russian journal"; the second, a bibliography of works by and about Bech, includes titles of bogus essays in real journals (*Commentary, Saturday Review* and *The New Republic,* to mention a few of them) by critics such as Alfred Kazin and Leslie Fiedler. The device does not harm the effectiveness of the primary fiction—the seven stories about Bech—but, in fact, provides the pleasant impression of an inside joke that the reader soon comprehends.

As in Updike's other novels, he gives himself a handicap in *Bech: A Book* and then strives to overcome it. In *The Poorhouse Fair,* it was the challenge to a young author to write empathetically about the aged; in *Couples,* to make obscene language and a confusing aggregate of people function artfully. In *Bech: A Book,* Updike the Protestant enters the preserve of the modern Jewish novelists. Not only does he choose to describe the innermost life of a Jew—an attempt rarely made by gentile authors—but selects a Jewish writer as hero, one whose personality, presumably, would be even more complex than that of a non-artist. Updike's characterization for the most part succeeds, both because he universalizes Bech's Jewishness into postures of authentic modern humanity in the manner of Saul Bellow's and Philip Roth's best writing and because he is careful to underplay the use of dialect and of the archetypal Jewish family and the Old World allusions that are the stock in trade of Bernard Malamud. Bech is an intellectual Jew (although not a Jewish intellectual), much more like Bellow's Moses Herzog than Malamud's Morris Bober.

It is tempting to project Bech as Updike's alter ego since certain superficial parallels exist, but the essential similarities are lacking. Updike, like Bech, has traveled to Eastern Europe on an officially sponsored cultural exchange tour; like Bech, he is at home in New England and New York; and, like Bech, he is in constant danger of losing his status as an independent artist and of submitting instead to cultural objectification, to the process whereby a contemporary artist becomes a static showpiece of the society he has sought to unsettle. But Bech is a "blocked" novelist, and Updike is not. After Bech has enjoyed some solid successes, enough and of such quality to make him a "major" writer in Updike's invented world, he has hit a sterile period— perhaps he has even written himself out. The single most consistent theme throughout the seven stories is Bech's frustrating inability to produce. It is a problem that Updike does not share; and, if Bech is in any significant way his alter ego, it must be only in the sense of incarnating the fear of impotence that any artist has.

Bech: A Book is different from Updike's previous fiction in the scope and nature of its humor. Hitherto, Updike had largely limited his use of humor to his poetry and to the satire collected in *Assorted Prose*; and he had reserved for his fiction a certain wit often more cynical than comic. *Bech* is sometimes quite funny, as if, in temporarily adopting a Jewish hero, Updike had also accepted the imperative of Jewish humor. Humor appears in the dialogue of *Couples,* it is true; but there its effect is radically weakened by the overriding awareness of guilt and death. *Bech: A Book* emits an attitude of liberation, as if its author had learned to endure some of life's enigmas and to smile at them. The brittleness of *The Music School* is gone, and a new relaxation has taken its place—even if the protagonist is as plagued and restless a man as George Caldwell in *The Centaur.*

II *The Seven Stories*

The first story, "Rich in Russia," is presented nominally as a lecture to a class of students regarding Bech's 1964 trip to the Soviet Union, where he is celebrated as an author of stature and given over fifteen hundred dollars' worth of rubles for Russian translations of his works. He tries hard to spend the rubles (apparently, he can't take the money out of the country); but he finds little to buy until, on the last day of his visit, he goes with Kate his translator to a Moscow shop and spends almost the whole sum for furs. As he hurries to catch his plane a short time later, his suitcase opens; and he drops furs, toys, and books on the runway. He and Kate, who is crying, gather them again; and he departs.

As the title suggests, the story turns on irony. Bech is indeed "rich in Russia," but he can't take the riches with him except in the form of exotic gifts. More than that, his richness is really personified in Kate, his loyal and emotional translator. When he kisses her at the airport, "he realized, horrified, that he should have slept with her." He has taken her and her dedication for granted; therefore, he has missed, more than a sexual encounter, the chance to know a valuable person well.

"Bech in Rumania," the second story, continues the novelist's cultural exchange tour of Eastern Europe. The counterpart to Kate in this tale is Petrescu, the translator who accompanies Bech on a trip to meet the head of the Rumanian Writers' Union. While on a sightseeing tour, Bech goes to a Bucharest performance of Eugene O'Neill's *Desire Under the Elms* and to a nightclub with another author ("the hottest Red writer this side of Solzhenitsyn") and his wife. Bech's conversations with Petrescu, combined with the running descriptions of life in modern Rumania as Bech sees it, comprise the essential story. The primary impression that results is the difficulty of communicating between two cultures. Bech and Petrescu like and respect each other, but a genuine friendship is thwarted by the lack of time and by the official busy-ness of the visit. The American Embassy people in Bucharest are enthusiastic bumblers, and the Rumanian leaders are rigid bureaucrats. The absence of rapport is epitomized by Bech's chauffeur, a taciturn Rumanian whose violent driving and constant hornblowing upset his passenger. The chauffeur seems to comprehend no English, yet he indicates at the end that he has indeed understood but has not tried to communicate. While on the plane leaving the country, Bech answers the unfamiliar words of a seatmate with "*Pardon, je ne comprends pas. Je suis Américain.*" The statement fits his whole · experience in the country, where "he realized that for four days he had been afraid." Bech thinks of himself "as a sort of low-flying U-2," as he tells an American from the Embassy; but his reconnaissance is not very effective on any level.

"The Bulgarian Poetess," winner of the First O. Henry Prize for 1966, is the first of Updike's stories to result from his 1964-1965 trip to Eastern Europe. In this tale, Bech arrives in Sofia, Bulgaria, for his last visit before returning to New York. Here he finds, unexpectedly, the "central woman"—the ideal he has always sought—in the person of a young poetess who arrives late to his reception. Although she is just as intensely attracted to him, they have only three brief meetings. At the last one, they exchange inscribed books (her poems and his novel) and separate, probably forever.

The success of the story depends not so much on the East-West romance theme as it does on the varied, repetitive use of mirror imagery that sustains the emotionality. How the mirror device works is described by Bech as he discusses the structure of his one good novel: "a counter-melody of imagery, interlocking images which had risen to the top and drowned his story." In Updike's story, the images of ghosts from Hawthorne's tale "Roger Malvin's Burial," the "shadow world" of the American embassies, the reflection from the polished table, the mirrors of the Moscow and Sofia ballets, and the Communists "behind the mirror" merge to suggest the enigmatic identity of the participants in the context of international tension. Bech's self-consciousness is dissolved in the encounter with Vera Glavanakova, the Bulgarian poetess; but his new sense of being remains intact only through the necessary separation from her.

"Bech Takes Pot Luck," the fourth story, reminds one a good deal of Saul Bellow's fiction and specifically of his protagonist Moses Herzog's strained living. Returned to the United States, Bech spends August on a Massachusetts island with his mistress, her sister, and the sister's children; but his vacation is interrupted by the appearance of one of his former students, named Wendell, from a Columbia University writing course. Bech and his mistress are not getting on well together, and the sister is suffering through a divorce. The young student enters the chaotic household and, through his ability to amuse the children and his general adeptness at beachfront living, provides some order and relief. When Norma, Bech's mistress, learns that the young man has L.S.D. at his apartment, she wants to try it; but he suggests that they smoke marijuana first "as a dry run." That evening, Bech, Norma, Beatrice the sister, and Wendell smoke the "grass." Nothing happens to Norma, but Bech becomes ill and vomits. Norma and Wendell drive away (to get rid of the L.S.D., it turns out, because Wendell feels guilty about Bech's nausea); and, in the interim, Bech and Beatrice establish a beginning intimacy. That night he sneaks away from Norma's bed to sleep with her sister, and "by fall the word went out on the literary circuit that Bech had shifted mistresses again."

The thrust of the story becomes clear through a consideration of the title's pun. The "pot luck" refers both to the drug and the sisters. Since Bech doesn't know how the indulgence will affect him, smoking "pot" becomes a matter of "pot luck." Furthermore, because of the marijuana, Norma and Wendell leave for a time, making it possible for Bech and Beatrice, both intoxicated, to set the stage for their affair; in that sense, pot luck is also at work. Pot luck also means taking whatever is offered, just as Bech accepts Beatrice's implicit offer of herself. However, the story does not capitalize on the drug vogue in order to achieve sensation but to integrate the theme. Certain traits of the characters are magnified, as if by the marijuana's influence, so that Updike can fit Norma's shrill greediness, Bech's aggressiveness, Beatrice's submission, and Wendell's naïveté into a pattern of contrived accident that marks another stage of the hero's restless career.

In "Bech Panics," Updike uses the framing device of a slide lecture (a narrator showing slides of Bech) to tell the story of Bech's performance as a lecturer at a Virginia girls' school. Now separated from Norma and involved with Bea, her sister, Bech is bothered by the two roles his new mistress plays as lover to him and as mother to her three young children; uncomfortable alone and with Bea, he alternates between his Riverside Drive apartment and her upstate New York home. From this ambivalence he flees in March to Virginia; but the abrupt transition to the rural college and pristine-looking girls, instead of relaxing him, instills a basic dread and an awareness of death that daze him. He undergoes an accelerated crisis of self-doubt, prays against his will, and then fulfills his duties as guest speaker. On the second evening, a young Jewish professor suggests that he sleep with her; but the slide-lecturer-as-narrator offers two versions of Bech's response. First, he says, Bech rejected her invitation and wept in front of the surprised woman. But then he says it is possible that Bech accepted the offer and sought to cure his spiritual sickness with her body. The next day Bech returns to New York and his uncomprehending mistress.

"Bech Panics" is, in terms of moral import, the profoundest story of the collection. Bech's temporary displacement, his retreat to the Virginia countryside, somehow makes him aware of the futility of language and reinforces his self-doubt; for his profession is that of language-craftsman. His fruitless argument with a black girl at the college, his artificial performance for the students, and the college poetry contest he is asked to judge emphasize the failure of language as a redemptive instrument. When alone in the woods between assignments, he prays a wordless prayer, however, and finds a measure of relief. As an ironic finale, Bech is taken to the airport by "a homely, tall, long-toothed woman" whose seductive drawl on the telephone had originally overcome his reluctance to travel to the campus. Words are deceptive, and the writer has to learn to accommodate deception without despair.

The story has a brutal and primitive undertone that contrasts with the genteel surface rhythms. Even the demure girls threaten Bech with a collective primal and smothering fertility, and his lovemaking with the young professor (if it indeed occurred) is described in grotesque anatomical terms. Bech panics because he has been shocked by rural nature out of the somnolent urban habits he has formed. He has nurtured his artist's impotence as a comfortable excuse to avoid facing squarely the dread of being, much as some neurotics love their illness; but his malingering is exposed by his new knowledge of the real problem—the need to locate meaning in an infinitely complex universe.

In "Bech Swings?," the novelist, now through with Bea, arrives in London to promote an English anthology of his writings. At a party he meets Merissa, a young and wealthy divorcée who takes him home with her. Without discovering much more about her or her background, he accompanies her in the ensuing evenings to a number of London's "mod" clubs, while on two day-time occasions he submits to an interview by a persistent and overly serious young American. Upon leaving London and flying back to New York, he reads a silly and pretentious *Observer* review by the American; but in a London tabloid he finds the column "Merissa's Week" (she is the daughter of the paper's owner) in which Merissa flatters him breezily as a man of the world.

The story begins with "Bech arrived in London with the daffodils," and Wordsworth's "I Wandered Lonely as a Cloud" becomes a central image. Bech is a lonely wanderer, and many things in springtime England remind him, in a melancholy way, of the season's gaiety celebrated in the Romantic's poem. Wordsworth's famous definition of poetic composition also figures in the tale. "The spontaneous overflow of powerful feelings ... from emotion recollected in tranquillity" does not work for Bech as a depiction of artistic creation or of lovemaking because, as Merissa reminds him in his impotence, he does not act "in tranquillity." Instead of developing a reflective creativity, Bech is becoming neurotically self-conscious. The narrator and Bech occasionally fuse, as particular descriptions by the narrator lodge in Bech's mind and become part of his compulsive phrasing. He articulates events while he experiences them, and he is so absorbed in introspective observation that he has little time for qualitative living. When Merissa in her gossip column reveals a perspective of him that he hadn't expected, he is charmed; but his pleasure is marred by the knowledge that he has once again played a role with her and has not revealed his authentic self. "He had become a character by Henry Bech" is the final sentence; the delusion of self-consciousness grows, and the shift from private novelist to celebrity seems complete.

The question mark of the title is important. Bech "swings" dubiously, not sure if he is enjoying or despairing. He is too self-aware for uninhibited participation, and the title carries the tone of proper incredulity even as it declares Bech's own intent.

"Bech Enters Heaven," the weakest story of the collection, is nonetheless an admirable display of wit. The story centers on two parallel episodes. In the first, when Bech is a precocious thirteen-year-old, he is taken from school by his mother one day to the northern end of Manhattan to attend a ceremony honoring literary luminaries. Young Bech is impressed. Years later, as a middle-aged novelist, he receives an invitation to attend a similar ceremony at which he himself is to be one of those honored. This gathering turns out to be a modern literary pantheon, a writers' heaven, into which Bech is formally admitted.

The tale is a parody both of Jewish-mother-and-son fiction and of the rituals by which America elevates and thereby ruins its artists. Mrs. Bech is ambitious for her son, and their visit to the ceremony is a crucial event that helps to formulate his vocational direction. The dialogue between the mother and boy does not ring quite true; but it sounds, understandably enough, like a gentile's imitation of Jewish-American diction and syntax. But artificiality does not seriously harm the story. If anything, it increases the hollowness of literary fame that Bech gains years later and the meaninglessness of the rites whereby such writers receive a sterile immortality. The final sentences are, "He had made it, he was here, in Heaven. Now what?" Even the ultimate achievement is cursed by boredom, and ennui pervades the pantheon.

III *The Success of Failure*

Bech is another in Updike's long line of protagonists who are complex failures, and nowhere do Updike's modern baroque tendencies show more clearly than in the intricacies of the hero-as-failure. Conner in *The Poorhouse Fair* is a bureaucratic success but a human failure; Harry Angstrom (before his *Rabbit Redux* maturation) is a sexual success but a total failure otherwise; George Caldwell is a social failure but a compassionate man; Joey Robinson is a failure as son, husband, and father; and the couples of Tarbox are all failures in love and friendship. Henry Bech is a social and cultural success; but, according to his own secret knowledge, he is a vocational failure—a bit of a "schlemiel," something of a *poseur,* a talented man who, spoiled by the selfish praise of a voracious society, has never fulfilled his promise. But one perceives more solid humanity in Bech than in all of Updike's previous heroes except George Caldwell. Bech is believable, likeable, and trustworthy. One senses in Updike's portrayal of him a new artistic toughness that may well mark the author's style in his prime.

CHAPTER 10

Rabbit Redux:
The Space beyond Myth

Kierkegaard smolders,/ But Eliot's ashes are dead.
—from "Thoughts While Driving Home"

I *Alternatives to Mythic Fiction*

IN *Couples* Updike uses myth to destroy itself, and through that novel he not only demythologizes *Eros* but also shows the possibility of demythologizing fiction itself. It is apparent that from now on fiction for Updike can be composed free of the help and weight of archetypal models, of vague secondary stories from the collective past. This liberation is necessary because the old strategy has become too transparent; we have become overly self-conscious about our mythicizing epistemology and have rendered the narration that depends on myth ineffective.

But how, then, does an author write mythless fiction? Updike tests some possibilities in *Bech: A Book*. There he works with current events, with fantasy as history, with a configuration of images, and with certain narrator tricks. The emphasis on contemporary world events and moods, already heavy in *Couples*, comes to the fore in the stories of Bech in Eastern Europe (in Bech's impressions of Russia, Bulgaria, Rumania) and in "Bech Takes Pot Luck" (through his participation in the emergent drug culture of the 1960's). The experiment with fantasy as history (Updike attempts the opposite, history as fantasy, in his long poem "Midpoint") introduces Bech as a real person rather than as a fictional figure, although Updike obviously does not expect anyone to accept Bech's actual existence. The orchestration of images replacing a dominant narrative line, a strategy Updike applies skillfully in "The Music School" story, dictates the structure of "The Bulgarian Poetess." The narrative-rhetorical tricks

operate in "Bech Panics" (an unidentified narrator relates the
story in the framework of a slide lecture) and in "Bech Swings?"
(Bech's musings merge with the narrator's imagery). Significantly, the only story relying on myth, "Bech Enters Heaven,"
is the single inferior tale in the collection.

In *Rabbit Redux* (the title means "Rabbit led back") Updike
settles on two of the alternatives to a fiction supported by myth:
on the stress on contemporary world events and on the orchestration of images.[1] He abandons the fantasy-as-history playfulness
entirely and limits the narrative-rhetorical tricks to one innova-
tion: the "reproduction" of news stories in rough form as they
appear on Rabbit's typesetting machine. The two alternatives
that he does develop basically contradict each other as modes
of structuring a novel. The accent on current events presupposes
a marked historical continuity in the book, but the emphasis
on image constellations suggests an ahistorical approach. Updike
not only reconciles these divergent tendencies; he makes them
reinforce each other to provide a unique fictive integrity that
replaces the old reliance on myth.

A conventional story line does inhabit *Rabbit Redux*. The time
is late July through October, 1969, ten years after the events of
Rabbit, Run. Harry Angstrom (no one has called him Rabbit for
years, although Updike still does) is now thirty-six, a typesetter;
he has grown politically conservative; and he is reunited with
his wife Janice. They live with their only child, the thirteen-
year-old Nelson, in Penn Villas, the new housing development
on the outskirts of Brewer, Pennsylvania. In the first chapter,
entitled "Pop/Mom/Moon," Harry learns that Janice is having
an affair with Stavros, a salesman of Greek descent who works
with her at her father's automobile sales lot. During a summer
weekend Rabbit and Janice have a confrontation regarding her
affair, after which she leaves him and Nelson to move in with
Stavros. On that Sunday afternoon Harry (with Nelson) visits
his parents in neighboring Mount Judge to celebrate his mother's
birthday. Old Mrs. Angstrom, now sixty-five, is slowly dying
of Parkinson's Disease. That night the four of them sit in the
sickroom and watch the television coverage of the first manned
moon landing.

In the second chapter, called "Jill," when Rabbit visits a local
black bar at the invitation of a Negro co-worker, he is maneuvered into taking home with him the eighteen-year-old runaway
rich girl Jill, whose white presence in the black community is

dangerous and awkward. Jill, a naïve radical idealist, becomes Harry's lover but also acts as a combined older sister and substitute mother for Nelson. Janice remains with Stavros even though he asks Harry to take her back. Harry's dying mother, who has always hated Janice, fights the possibility of a new reconciliation.

In the third chapter, "Skeeter," Harry arrives home from work one day to find that Jill has taken in a young Negro, a Vietnam veteran called Skeeter who has jumped bail following a drugs-dealing charge and who proclaims himself to be the black Jesus. He becomes a contentious member of the strange household, makes love to Jill, supplies her with increasingly stronger drugs, and seeks to give Harry an education in black history, radical politics, and an anti-Establishment life style. Rabbit gradually succumbs. He smokes marijuana nightly with Jill and Skeeter and also absorbs (with Nelson sitting in) their arguments about the immorality of the Vietnam war and about the exploitative and repressive nature of modern American society. One night they are spied on from outside as Jill and Skeeter are sexually involved. Rabbit has already been warned by two neighbors to disperse his shocking ménage or suffer the consequences. On a Saturday night soon after, while he and Nelson are visiting the divorcée Peggy Fosnacht and her son, Rabbit receives a call from Skeeter urging him to come home. They return to find the house in flames. Jill, probably in a doped sleep, dies in the fire in spite of Nelson's frantic pleas to save her. Early the next morning Harry finds Skeeter and drives him out of town to aid his escape from the searching police.

In the final chapter, "Mim," Harry and Nelson have moved in with Harry's parents in Mount Judge. Harry loses his job with the declining Verity Press. When his sister Mim, now a high-priced call girl on the West Coast, comes east for a visit, she in her tough way reorganizes the lives of her relatives. She not only encourages Rabbit toward a reunion with Janice but also expedites it by sleeping with Stavros. After Janice has helped Stavros through a terrifying heart seizure one night, she, in a spirit of confused self-sacrifice (she fears that their affair will kill him), decides to leave him at last. She and Rabbit meet at their gutted Penn Villas house, drive to a motel, and, without making love, sleep together.

II *The Orchestration of Tropes*

Such a narrative summation reads like a caricature because the story line of *Rabbit Redux* is mainly a vehicle of orientation in a work of fiction that succeeds by other means. The novel is crucially aligned to historical world events. Some are specifically datable, such as the first manned moon flight and landing, the race riots in York and Reading (Pennsylvania), and the Chappaquiddick drowning of Mary Jo Kopechne with its repercussions on Senator Edward Kennedy's political career. Others are continuous: the Vietnam war, the increasing drugs traffic, the growing polarization of segments of American society, and the deterioration of the cities. All of these merge with the orchestration of images to give the book its substance.

The trope of space and space-exploration images is dominant. It is displayed literally in the fragments of recorded conversation from American astronauts and Russian cosmonauts during space flights and dockings that prefix each of the four sections; in the depiction of the televised moon landing that Rabbit and his relatives watch; and in the account of Rabbit, Janice, and Nelson in a movie theater viewing Stanley Kubrick's *2001: A Space Odyssey*. These references act as the context for metaphoric uses of space. The maneuvers of space docking provide the background for images of security and physical contact. The spectral figures of the astronauts on the moon set the tone for the strong ghost imagery, which stands for the insubstantial quality of American life and for the haunting memory of better times. The phenomenon of floating free in space becomes the basis for images of Janice's liberation from Rabbit, of sexual excitement, or of drug-inspired sensations. The spaciousness of space offers an ironic counterpart to the images of density in the black ghettos and in American cities generally.

The space-docking maneuver underlies many scenes. For example, Harry is thinking of his mother while riding home from work: "Rabbit's mind, as the bus dips into its bag of gears and surges and shudders, noses closer into the image of her." At the critical moment, when Jill and Skeeter—her head between his thighs—are spied through a window, they seem to Rabbit "an interlocked machine." The final scenes of the book, ones in which Harry and Janice cautiously reconcile and sleep together in the Safe Haven Motel, are done in forthright space coupling imagery: "he and she seem to be slowly revolving, afraid of jarring one another away"; and, "In a space of silence, he can't gauge how much, he feels them drift along sideways deeper into being married."

The apparition-like figures of the astronauts on the moon, as transmitted by television, are the natural models for ghost metaphors and sensations. Janice sees Rabbit as "a ghost, white, soft." Jill, wan and "transparent," seems ghostly to Rabbit and appears as a ghost in his bedroom some weeks after her death. Old Mrs. Angstrom is a "shade" and an "apparition"; Rabbit calls Skeeter a "spook." Rabbit dreams of a spectral white city; his mother dreams of him and Mim as ghosts. The condition of floating free is reworked metaphorically as Janice masturbates and thinks of herself as "Floating now like a ballerina among the sparse planets of her life"; and as Rabbit, coming home with Jill after smoking marijuana ("This smoky creature at his side has halved his weight"), "floats up the steps to the porchlet." The ironic opposite of immense space is the cramped space of Mount Judge and Brewer and the lack of physical and spiritual room that Skeeter as black man feels.

A second trope, almost as pervasive as the space trope, deals in a great variety of underwater imagery. Its historical bases are the United States-Russian agreement to ban atomic weapons from the ocean floor and the drowning of Mary Jo Kopechne. Its fictive orientation is Janice's drowning of the baby Becky in *Rabbit, Run*. Employed metaphorically, it serves many dimensions of the novel. Old Mrs. Angstrom has nightmares of drowning; Skeeter has Nelson read an "underwater" passage from William Lloyd Garrison (*"let the Republic sink beneath the waves of oblivion . . ."*); Jill, indulging in oral sex, is "like a little girl bobbing for apples"; when Harry supports the sickened Nelson during the fire in which Jill burns, "He is holding him up from drowning. If Harry were to let go, he would drown too."

Other tropes contribute to the fundamental organization of the novel. The persistent black-white trope, based on contemporary race relations, incarnates more specifically the relation between Rabbit and Skeeter and between Skeeter and Jill; it also underscores the oversimplifications of Rabbit's thinking, in which things are "black and white" with no shades of gray; and it stresses the urgent tangibility of America's problems versus its transparent solutions. The winged-figure trope, which harks back to Janice's feeling that a third person is in the room when Becky drowns, is prominent. When Rabbit talks to Janice by telephone, he "sees her wings hover, her song suspended: imagines himself soaring, rootless, free." Rabbit masturbates lying on his stomach because he feels God is over him, "spreading His feathered wings as above a crib." When Stavros has his seizure, Janice again feels "a third person in the room"; and when Harry and Janice are in bed in the motel, "All sorts of winged presences exert themselves in the air above their covers." The mirror trope, which continues to fascinate Updike, provides images of attempts at reciprocal understanding (in "The Bulgarian Poetess" it serves as an odd adjunct to the "reflection" theories of Marx and Lenin). Harry sees himself reflected by Peggy Fosnacht; Jill explains God, spirit, and matter to Nelson through mirror analogies; Harry observes obliquely (through mirrors) what he fears to see directly: his house afire and Skeeter. Effective are also the Jesus trope (Harry's last minutes with Skeeter are filled with Jesus symbolism); the basketball trope (Harry explains the Vietnam war as "a kind of head fake. To keep the other guy off balance"); and the Peter Rabbit trope (Rabbit sneezes at critical moments, like Peter Rabbit in Mr. MacGregor's garden).

The tropes function not only individually to provide an imagistic consistency and continuity throughout the novel; they also merge, blending in and out of each other, to produce a sense of interconnectedness and interchangeability that gives the book its integrity and vast allusiveness. Moreover, the "big" subjects of war, sex, violence, space exploration, drugs, America's polarization and loss of self-confidence are related better than ever to the Middle American milieu in Updike's writing through the orchestration of tropes. For example, early in the novel, Janice and Rabbit make love in the light of the television screen, "by the bluish flicker of module models pantomiming flight, of riot troops standing before smashed supermarkets, of a rowboat landing in Florida having crossed the Atlantic, of situation comedies and western melodramas, of great gray momentary faces unstable as quicksilver." But this scene also mingles images of ghosts, mirrors, black and white, Peter Rabbit, and space exploration. The realistic background and the network of tropes merge, then, in a description in which Janice's body becomes simultaneously the newly discovered moonscape and a Vietnam battlefield. In mid-novel, when Rabbit, Jill, Skeeter, and Nelson engage in an acute political-cultural discussion about race relations and America's future, Updike creates a mélange of space, underwater, black-white, Jesus, mirrors, and winged-figures tropes. In the concluding motel scene the tropes and images of space coupling, floating in space, ghosts, winged figures, Peter Rabbit, and black-white interact.

The immensely intricate interplay of tropes—a further refinement of the "secular baroque" that designs Updike's fiction—produces an effect like that of a long and complex poem, and yet the novel's traditional domain of fictive historicity is not lost. It is caught up and transformed by the imagistic effort, while the story line itself, although outdone by the tropes' effects, is still sufficiently assertive to prevent the novel from becoming a pseudopoem. *Rabbit Redux* is not grounded in history and reinforced by fictive imagery; it is based on the imagery and is reinforced by history.

Hence the novel, for all of its absorption in contemporary problems, does not become social propaganda but diffuses its concern through esthetic channels. The sense of the disintegrating quality of American life in the 1960's is transmitted not only by the image clusters (ghosts, drowning, the emptiness of space, the tension of black and white) but also by references to nostalgia and by expressions of banality. Updike has always excelled at evoking nostalgia. In *Rabbit Redux* he recalls the Lone Ranger, Big Little Books, old pop tunes, children's games on summer evenings, and the vital centers of small towns before the shopping malls destroyed them; the recollection, however, is not intended to create the pleasant ache for lost good times but to shape a framework for comprehending the drastic nature of modern America's deterioration. The present contrasts with the "decades when Americans moved within the American dream, laughing at it, starving on it, but living it, humming it, the national anthem everywhere. . . . Rabbit had come in on the end of it, as the world shrank like an apple going bad and America was no longer the wisest hick town within a boat ride of Europe."

This novel lacks the liberal-redemptive presence of a Reverend Eccles who, a key figure in *Rabbit, Run*, is not even alluded to here. Instead, Updike prefigures the second section with the inane remark of a space hero—Neil Armstrong saying, "It's different but it's very pretty out here"—and intensifies the climate of banality with details of MacDonald's hamburger stands, shoddy motels, and neon-ornamented bars. The magnificence of outer space is tempered by the tawdriness of Middle America; the potential tragedy of the characters' lives is undone by their vulgarities.

III *Instructive Motion*

Above all, *Rabbit Redux* is effectively vulgar and sometimes even efficiently perverse; a decade ago it would have been considered obscene. Its attentiveness to the sounds, tastes, and smells of sexual union along with the usual visual-tactile description; its matter-of-fact treatment of promiscuity; and its use of a sexual-profane language publicly taboo a generation ago render it offensive by traditional standards, but its "obscenity" is precisely directed. Copulation, its variations, and its vocabulary are an expression of outraged sensibility, an indulgence in the very irresponsibility that provokes outrage, and a refuge from the exhausting personal-social reality that condones both the outrage and its causes. Little lyric sex animates the book, much less than appears in *Couples*: the sexual exercises in *Rabbit Redux* usually have an ulterior purpose. Skeeter exerts a revenge on Jill's body for what he perceives as the white man's humiliation of his race; Jill makes love to Rabbit in lieu of paying rent, as a protest against her parents' wealthy-wasteful existence, and also as a sensual catharsis that provides temporary relief from her teenaged intellectual and emotional confusion; Rabbit copulates with Jill as a substitute for his wife and with Peggy Fosnacht (on the night of the fire) as a social obligation. Janice appropriates her lover's body to celebrate and assert her discovery of feminine identity; and, Mim, who has made sex a profession and a life style, not only sells her body but also derives her pragmatic values from her call girl experiences.

The novel does not exploit sex for its sensation value; there is still less ground for that charge against *Rabbit Redux* than against *Couples*. Instead, nostalgia, banality, vulgarity, and obscenity combine to establish the atmosphere of national deterioration; but they are also a cause of the deterioration. Updike's America is now afflicted by a longing for the security of the romanticized past that seems in contradiction to the adventurous, futuristic spirit imperative to the space-age mentality; the country is cursed by a poverty of the imagination and by a vulgarity of taste that betray its former high-minded hopes and intentions; it is pervaded by an obscenity that dehumanizes relationships on every level and that exposes the great cost of technological triumph. In this sad situation the personal and political positions of Left, Right, and Center are all equally ineffective, yet it is instructive to follow Rabbit's journey toward increasing political awareness, for it is not wasted motion.

In *Rabbit Redux* Harry Angstrom undergoes a quest, a seduction, a conversion, and an education. This sequel to *Rabbit, Run* is also a quest novel, but it has neither the mythic dimension of the quest that the earlier book had nor the willing participation of the protagonist in the quest. Rabbit at twenty-six, ten years younger, saw himself gladly as a spiritual searcher, even though he was too naïve to understand himself as representative of the American effort of the 1950's to escape a paralyzing ennui. In that novel his self-image of the searcher is also a convenient disguise for the immaturity and lust that really direct his behavior. Now, approaching middle age, he has become sedentary and is a reluctant quester. The threat of change has already turned him reactionary, and he resists the rapid and perplexing transformations in American society. In *Rabbit, Run* he is the restless quester among those who wish him to remain constant; in *Rabbit Redux* he is the stubborn conservative among those who urge change. In the early novel, ironically, for all of his struggle to change, he cannot; in the sequel, ironically, for all of his struggle to remain the same, he changes.

Rabbit's seduction-and-conversion experiences recall a text of the theology student's sermon in the short story "Lifeguard": "Every seduction is a conversion." Updike introduces the third section of the novel with the words of a "Background Voice Aboard Soyuz 5": "We've been raped, we've been raped!" and indeed, this part of *Rabbit Redux* plays with ravishment. Jill is "raped" by Skeeter (she takes pleasure in the game of violation) while Rabbit reads them, at Skeeter's request, a brutal passage from *The Life and Times of Frederick Douglass* about black slave-woman and white-master relations. Later that night Skeeter masturbates while Harry finishes the passage, and Harry almost yields to the lure of homosexuality. But the crux of his seduction and conversion is not sexual; the sexuality, along with the marijuana and the evening readings and talks, is mainly an instrument that gradually draws Rabbit away from his defense of America's moral superiority and toward a negative-critical view of his country's history and present state. In the process, his privacy and his house are violated and his son exposed to corrupting influence, but Harry is also to blame, since he does not resist these infringements. Tricked into taking Jill and Skeeter into his household, he accepts them with a good-natured hospitality mixed with curiosity and fear. His seduction is by them, and his conversation is more a personal response to them than a change of mind or heart.

Of what, then, does Harry's education consist? His lessons are at last neither political nor sociological but personal. More exactly, they are political and sociological ones corrected by decisive personal experience. Rabbit's drift to the left is characterized by acts of radical apolitical behavior—giving refuge to a runaway rich girl and a bail jumper, as well as smoking illegal narcotics—and not at all by political activity. In fact, returned to his parents' home after Jill's death, he again defends the necessity of the Vietnam war to his sister. But he does learn. He learns, a bit, to reflect and to react less on visceral reflex. He learns the advantages of enduring in a marriage, of accepting the subtly deepening and unifying dimensions of its daily routine rather than expecting the excitement of a lover. He learns to forgive, and to function while suffering. In sum, he acquires, no doubt belatedly, a fair degree of maturity and emerges not as the despicable fugitive of the *Rabbit, Run* conclusion but as a man who has asserted himself in the midst of overwhelming personal weaknesses and social confusion and gained a measure of dignity thereby.

The "redux" of the novel's title has connotations of recovery from illness that come to apply spiritually to Harry. He has been a ghost, a Peter Rabbit, a mirror image, an underwater struggler, a space drifter, and a victim of a demonic Jesus; but he survives all these to choose, beyond them, a new start with his partner in guilt, shame, and promise. Although he has been sent on a quest against his will, he performs, if not gracefully, at least with a humanity that has an aura of grace. Thus, whereas *Rabbit, Run* stops with the quest dissolved into physical panic ("he runs. Ah: runs. Runs"), the end of *Rabbit Redux* is a resolution of quietness and equanimity: "He. She. Sleeps. O.K.?"

IV *The Social Impact of Fictive Risks*

Few novelists would dare to conclude a long and serious novel with "O.K." Fewer still could make that slangy word carry the accumulated weight of emotional meaning that Updike gives it. The ending of *Rabbit Redux* reminds one of Updike's fondness for gimmickry and of his ability to convert the gimmick into fine art. *Rabbit Redux* makes more use of gimmicks than any of his previous novels; he takes more risks than ever before, yet one never has a sense of precarious artistry. He has become such a master at solving problems of fictive technique that the risks look calculated when they are not. They are genuine. Updike has erected almost flagrantly difficult obstacles for himself and has overcome them, not merely for the sake of meeting the challenge (although one guesses that this aspect fascinates him), but to create the superior literature resulting from the imaginative realignments that his risks generate.

Updike writes *Rabbit Redux* in the historical present, as he did *Rabbit, Run,* and the effects of that technique reinforce the continuation of the earlier novel's action. The composition of a sequel, however, is a strategy belonging to an outmoded tradition of novel writing, one associated nowadays with inferior fiction. Not only must Updike offset the negative overtones of sequel fiction; he must also develop an unpromising protagonist, for Harry Angstrom at the close of *Rabbit, Run* looks like dead-end material. Updike makes the momentum of the earlier novel work for him. The small-city atmosphere of Brewer is perfect for framing the urban, racial, and moral crises of the new book. Rabbit's own evolution from an irresponsible and romantic drifter to lower-middle-class conservative and patriot is entirely credible. His characterization in *Rabbit Redux* is a brilliant coup on Updike's part that makes a familiar figure reusable and, like the locale, dramatizes the varieties of crisis.

A sequel, carefully handled, is an ideal vehicle for stressing both continuity and change. *Rabbit Redux* not only conveys both but also shows how they relate. The absence of deep beliefs, of strong traditions, or of a sustaining vision accompanies and sharpens the tangible problems of America, increases its self-doubt, and causes antagonism among its citizens. In such situations some fall back on the superficial creeds of national infallibility and messianic mission, reasserting the old values with vehemence, while others assume a supercritical posture and belittle the old values and their modern consequences. One seeks security either in continuity or in change. *Rabbit, Run* was successful in the early 1960's, among other reasons, because it showed Rabbit as a sad caricature of the American dreamer. Between that novel and its sequel the very dream has disintegrated; America has become a caricature of its old self. Rabbit, now caught in the tension between continuity and change, between a stubborn worship of the dream and a firsthand experience of its dissolution, is not the substance of the caricature in *Rabbit Redux* but the one who absorbs and reflects it. In this capacity he is just as apt an agent for registering the mood of the late 1960's and beyond as he was for the decade of *Rabbit, Run*. Through him, Updike makes the composition of a sequel seem not only plausible but almost requisite.

The schizoid and paranoid symptoms of the polarized nation that Harry exhibits are magnified in Skeeter, whose characterization is the second gimmick-risk in *Rabbit Redux*. Updike's empathetic capacity is well known. In his first novel, he extrapolates skillfully from the consciousness of aged people; in *Bech: A Book*, he writes from the imagined perspective of a Jewish artist, inviting a comparison of his imitation with the originals by prominent Jewish authors. The depiction of an amoral, crazy Negro offered in the context of the volatile contemporary racial situation is the most audacious yet of Updike's experiments with borrowed voices. Judged by normal, logical standards, Skeeter is scarcely a believable character. His experiential, emotional, and prophetic capacities are too rich for a single person and tempt one to regard him as a type rather than as an individual. As Vietnam war veteran turned antiwar, drugs dealer, self-proclaimed revolutionary, and black messiah, he is an incarnation of the fearful shapes that have transformed the American dream into a nightmare. Because Skeeter is too powerful a creation for the otherwise realistic cast of the novel, his portrayal threatens to unbalance the whole artistic effort. But one must grant his viability as a credible individual and not only as a type when one recognizes that he is as he is for sound psychological and social reasons. His schizophrenia is manifested in his fragmented (not only split but fragmented) personality, in his manic but futile attempts to integrate his real and ideal identities as traumatized war veteran, minor criminal, seducer and lover, racial avenger and redeemer. He lives his paranoia in fear of white persecution and in the delusion of grandeur as self-styled savior.

Because both of Skeeter's illnesses have social dimensions and explicit social causes, one cannot dismiss them as merely personal psychoses. The schizophrenic strain is national, perhaps global, and is particularly virulent in Skeeter because he has been subjected to it in so many roles: as black man in a white society, as soldier in a controversial war, and as a sensitive person in a callous world. His paranoiac fears have some basis in fact: he is indeed sought after by the police, the object of a plot to trap him and others. But instead of suggesting that the social grounds for Skeeter's sickness should excuse him, in the fashion of the Naturalist novelists—he remains a culpable character, especially after allowing Jill's death—Updike reveals through him the epidemic nature of his malaise. Skeeter is unbelievable when judged against the old patterns of reality, but he is an embodiment of newer forms of it. He may appear to be an exaggeration, but the new patterns often partake of excess, and, seen in those terms, Skeeter is both a fitting example of the modern hyperexperience and a conceivable product of it.

A third gimmick is the interpolation of special typeset paragraphs in the narrative. The paragraphs are typographically distinct from the rest of the novel; done in the "blacker" and denser newspaper style, they include mistakes of individual letters, words, and lines as well as their corrections. Updike integrates this anomalous aspect into the remainder of the book by linking it to Harry's job as a typesetter. The passages that Harry composes in type for *The Brewer Vat* relate to the dominant tropes of the book, to its plot, and to Harry's interior monologue as he works. Beyond that unifying function, the typeset paragraphs show Harry's transitional cognitive process and the mutability of language itself. Harry, a professional typesetter and an avid newspaper reader, is a Gutenberg man; he is at home with the linear thought and with the sequential action to which the printed page has accustomed him. As a conservative, he thinks not only within the framework of the old content of Western society but also, naturally enough, in terms of its patterns. But, influenced by television, he has started to change even before his seduction and responds to the increasing vocality of the electronic age, to its multi-sensuous impressions, to its illusions of simultaneous activity, to the tendency of its inhabitants to suspend final judgments. Janice says of him, "He put his life into rules he feels melting away now. I mean, I know he thinks he's missing something, he's always reading the paper and watching the news." He handles his typesetter like a computer and foreshadows thereby the fate of his nearly obsolete machine and of his job.

Other graphic devices in the novel—capital letters to signify the titles on moviehouse marquees, graffiti drawn with spray paint on Rabbit's gutted home, or Jill's literally hand-drawn peace and love symbols—show language degenerating into slogans. Like Rabbit himself, language is enslaved by technology but also naïvely resisting it. "All around him, Rabbit hears language collapsing." Updike, via his typographical innovations, calls attention to the crisis of language in the throes of transition.

V *Transcendent Fiction*

Rabbit Redux, as one reviewer commented, is the work of "an awesomely accomplished writer," but Updike's brilliance is almost the book's undoing.[2] Although the action and the imagery are reinforced by contemporary history, the narrative proclaims such a self-contained artistic reality that it threatens to break away from experienced life and show itself, splendid and inaccessible like a space vehicle, from a remote distance. Its near-flawlessness tends to alienate. Harry's fight with Janice, his fist fight with Skeeter, and the fire that kills Jill, for instance, are scenes of intended emotional intensity so perfectly rendered that they nearly become esthetic curiosities: the reader stops to admire and analyze them but does not yield to unselfconscious involvement in the fictive illusion. Yet one must recall that this is fiction beyond myth that demands a different quality of response: it asks one to maintain a double vision—to keep in mind even during the imagination's exercises that the fictive illusion *is* an illusion, although a necessary one. This illusion models possibilities of existence in order to help one avoid and select.

This double vision, this balancing between reality and illusion, can too easily slip into a schizophrenia of the sort that Updike portrays in *Rabbit Redux,* but it need not. His secular baroque is also a double vision but a positive and affirmative one that is dependent on negative capability—on the ability to remain creatively critical in times of great confusion. Updike's venture beyond myth is not a denial of the imagination but an indication of increased reliance on it. *Rabbit Redux* not only confirms the maturation of Updike as artist but also contributes to the maturation of fiction itself. As a novel, it transcends the tradition of the novel in order to help generate new, and better, styles of being.

is spectacular; and his shaping of structure is so smooth and unobtrusive that his mastery often goes unperceived. He is an expert in assigning and developing narrative point of view, in fashioning dialogue with a minimum of stage direction, and in utilizing stream-of-consciousness passages to convey the temper of crucial times and places. He has been successful in discovering effective substitutes for traditional formula fiction. As a stylist, then, he is anything but out of date. Indeed, he pushes constantly beyond the old techniques he has mastered in order to mold new experience with new methods.

Updike has said that he is "kind of elegiacally concerned with the Protestant middle class," a statement implying his awareness of this era's decline.[1] Two aspects of his fiction carry the sense of an age passing. In the short stories, it is the hyper-self-conscious stance; the intensely introspective attitude is both an expression of ill health and an effort to effect a cure. In the novels, the decline is handled through the ironic use of myth, the demythologizing tendency, and the search for a reality beyond myth. Above all, Updike manipulates myths toward self-destruction to make the reader realize that the old institutions they reflect are disintegrating. Nostalgia results, for he is reluctant to see the era disappear.

But it would be short-sighted to consider Updike as merely a novelist of transition. He is still a relatively young man, perhaps just now in mid-career. Already a major writer in terms of quality and production, he has shown more than sufficient versatility and flexibility to perform well in a more unequivocal future—not as a prophet of the Apocalypse (in which event fiction would not matter), nor as the proclaimer of a new technological Utopia—as a witness to the enduring and gradually transforming power of good craftsmanship as a primary humanizing force. Updike is not as radically committed to art-as-salvation as is his character Peter Caldwell in *The Centaur*. Young Caldwell the painter has maneuvered himself into a situation in which nothing *can* help him but his art, but Updike has retained options. Since he has not divorced himself from the middle-class institutions and customs, he can function with a certain degree of relaxation that allows him to concentrate on craftsmanship. He does not allow the urgency of world crises or even the inherent dramatic power of the so-called great themes to dictate his writing (not even in *Rabbit Redux*) but persists in a meticulous, patient molding of the nuances that gradually accrue to constitute the substance of daily life. In Updike's art one finds a direct relationship between the quality of craftsmanship and the quality of life: by doing a thing well, one creates a better self.

Updike is above all a believer in vocation, and he uses in his own "calling" a passive and active voice. He embodies the skill and confidence of the professional who is, in himself, an orienting point in a perplexed world. But the sum effect of his fiction is to impress his readers directly with the conviction that, although things are not good, men can still work meaningfully to make them so.

Notes and References

Chapter One

1. The poetry introducing Chapters 1-6 appears in John Updike, *Telephone Poles and Other Poems* (New York, 1963); the poetry introducing Chapters 7, 8, and 11 is taken from John Updike, *The Carpentered Hen and Other Tame Creatures* (New York, 1958); the lines introducing Chapter 9 are taken from John Updike, *Midpoint and Other Poems* (New York, 1969).

2. *Olinger Stories* (New York, 1964), vii. The eleven stories in this collection appear also in *The Same Door, Pigeon Feathers,* and *The Music School.* The only new material in *Olinger Stories* is Updike's brief introduction.

3. The Maples also appear in the following short stories: "Marching Through Boston," *The New Yorker* (January 22, 1966); "Your Lover Just Called," *Harper's* (January, 1967); "The Taste of Metal," *The New Yorker* (March 11, 1967); "Eros Rampant," *Harper's* (June, 1968).

Chapter Two

1. *Assorted Prose* (New York, 1965), p. 156.
2. *Ibid.*
3. *Ibid.*, p. 306.

Chapter Three

1. Updike has said that he passed through an acute religious crisis during the time he was writing *Rabbit, Run,* and some of that crisis is reflected in the novel. Cf. "View from the Catacombs," *Time,* XCI (April 26, 1968), 74.

Chapter Four

1. *Olinger Stories,* ix.
2. *Ibid.*

Chapter Five

1. Arthur Mizener, *The Sense of Life in the Modern Novel* (Boston, 1964), pp. 264ff.
2. Wylie Sypher, *Rococo to Cubism in Art and Literature* (New York: Vintage Books, 1960), pp. 295ff.
3. *Ibid.*, p. 301.

4. Philip Rieff, *The Triumph of the Therapeutic* (New York: Harper & Row, 1966).

5. Mircea Eliade, *Cosmos and History: The Myth of the Eternal Return* (New York: Harper & Row, 1959). Cf. Chapter Four, "The Terror of History."

Chapter Six

1. John Thompson, "Matthiessen and Updike, *The New York Review of Books*, VII (December 23, 1965), 23.

Chapter Eight

1. Some representative reviews of *Couples* are William H. Gass, "Cock-a-doodle-doo," *The New York Review of Books*, X (April 11, 1968), 3; Alfred Kazin, "Updike: Novelist of the New, Post-pill America," *The Washington Post Book World*, II (April 7, 1968), 1, 3; and Granville Hicks, "God Has Gone, Sex is Left," *Saturday Review*, LI (April 6, 1968), 21-22. Hicks states that Piet Hanema is unlike Updike in that Piet has never gone to college; but on p. 19 of *Couples* one reads that Piet was a sophomore at Michigan State University when his parents were killed in an automobile accident.

2. "View from the Catacombs," 66.

3. A church did burn down in Updike's town of Ipswich prior to his composition of *Couples*; the destruction of the Congregational Church in Tarbox is not a tenuous symbolic event but is inspired by an actual occurrence. The clichés of art are sometimes modeled on the clichés of life.

4. "More Love in the Western World," *Assorted Prose*, pp. 283-300.

5. *Ibid.*, p. 298.

6. *Ibid.*, p. 286.

7. *Ibid.*, p. 291.

8. *Ibid.*, p. 299.

Chapter Ten

1. Sections of the first chapter of *Rabbit Redux* were published as "Pop/Mom/Moon" in *The Atlantic*, CCXXVIII (August, 1971), 48-51, 54-63; and as "Rabbit's Evening Out" in *Esquire*, LXXVI (September, 1971), 109-12, 191-96. The novel itself was published in November, 1971.

2. Anatole Broyard, "Updike Goes All Out at Last," *The New York Times*, Vol. CXXI (November 5, 1971), 40.

Chapter Eleven

1. "View from the Catacombs," 66.

Selected Bibliography

Updike's life, like his fiction, seems suited to a simultaneous exploitation and destruction of myth and also to an extremely self-conscious encounter with reality. He was born in 1932 in Shillington, Pennsylvania, the only child of Wesley and Linda Grace Hoyer Updike. When he was thirteen the family moved to his grandparents' farm in Plowville, ten miles outside of Shillington. He and his father, a high school science teacher, commuted to the Shillington public schools. His adolescence was austere and isolated, but he was encouraged by his literary-minded mother to develop his writing talents and to grow into a vocation that would take him beyond the confines of the rural Pennsylvania Dutch community.

A good student, Updike went from Shillington to Harvard, where he majored in English, edited the Harvard *Lampoon*, and was graduated *summa cum laude* in 1954. Between his junior and senior years he married Mary Pennington, whom he had met while she was a fine arts major at Radcliffe. After his graduation they spent a year in Oxford at the Ruskin School of Drawing and Fine Arts; and, upon returning to the United States, he was employed as a staff writer for *The New Yorker*. He held that position and lived with his family in Manhattan for two years, then moved with them in 1957 to Ipswich, Massachusetts. By 1959, following the publication of *The Same Door* and *The Poorhouse Fair*, he was becoming nationally known as a writer. The publication of *Rabbit, Run* in 1960 enhanced that reputation greatly; since then, on the strength of his productivity and the high quality of his prose, he has become accepted as one of America's major living novelists.

Little of the old-style literary legend informs Updike's private life. He is a steady worker who writes during regular hours in an Ipswich office; he is a family man, the father of two sons and two daughters; he is accessible to reporters and to seekers-after-advice; but he is not a "public" figure *à la* Norman Mailer or Truman Capote. Reared a Unitarian among Lutherans and Mennonites in Eastern Pennsylvania, Updike has not abandoned institutional religion; but he has become a member of the Congregational Church in Ipswich. In short, although he is hardly a representative middle-class citizen, he does participate in many facets of the middle-class life that is also the subject of his fiction.

Much personal reminiscence appears in the "First Person Singular"

173

essays of Updike's *Assorted Prose*. It is excellent writing and often reads as well as his fiction.

Two bibliographies of Updike have been published to date:

TAYLOR, C. CLARKE. *John Updike: A Bibliography*. Kent, Ohio: Kent State University Press, 1968. A thorough, annotated work that contains entries through 1966.

SOKOLOFF, B. A. *Comprehensive Bibliography of John Updike*. Darby, Pennsylvania: Darby Books, 1970.

PRIMARY SOURCES

1. Novels and Collected Fiction

The Poorhouse Fair. New York: Alfred A. Knopf, 1958.
The Same Door. New York: Alfred A. Knopf, 1959.
Rabbit, Run. New York: Alfred A. Knopf, 1960.
Pigeon Feathers. New York: Alfred A. Knopf, 1962.
The Centaur. New York: Alfred A. Knopf, 1963.
Olinger Stories. New York: Vintage, 1964.
Of the Farm. New York: Alfred A. Knopf, 1965.
The Music School. New York: Alfred A. Knopf, 1966.
Couples. New York: Alfred A. Knopf, 1968.
Bech: A Book. New York: Alfred A. Knopf, 1970.
Rabbit Redux. New York: Alfred A. Knopf, 1971.

2. Selected Uncollected Short Fiction

"Marching through Boston," *The New Yorker*, XLI (January 22, 1966), 34-38.
"Museums and Women," *The New Yorker*, XLIII (November 18, 1967), 57-61.
"The Wait," *The New Yorker*, XLIV (February 17, 1968), 34-96.
"Eros Rampant," *Harper's*, CCXXXV (June, 1968), 59-64.
"The Day of the Dying Rabbit," *The New Yorker*, XLV (August 30, 1969), 22-26.
"The Deacon," *The New Yorker*, XLVI (February 21, 1970), 38-41.
"The Orphaned Swimming Pool," *The New Yorker*, XLVI (June 27, 1970), 30-32.

3. Collected Discursive Prose

Assorted Prose. New York: Alfred A. Knopf, 1965.

4. Selected Uncollected Reviews

"Death's Heads," *The New Yorker*, XLI (October 2, 1965), 216-28.
"The Author as Librarian," *The New Yorker*, XLI (October 30, 1965), 223-46.
"The Fork," *The New Yorker*, XLII (February 26, 1966), 115-34.
"Questions Concerning Giacomo," *The New Yorker*, XLIV (April 6, 1968), 167-74.
"Fool's Gold," *The New Yorker*, XLVI (August 8, 1970), 72-76.

5. Collected Poetry

The Carpentered Hen and Other Tame Creatures. New York: Harper & Row, Publishers, 1958.
Telephone Poles and Other Poems. New York: Alfred A. Knopf, 1963.
A Child's Calendar. New York: Alfred A. Knopf, 1965.
Verse. Greenwich, Connecticut: Fawcett, 1965.
Midpoint and Other Poems. New York: Alfred A. Knopf, 1969.

6. Adaptations

The Magic Flute by Wolfgang Amadeus Mozart. John Updike and Warren Chappell (adaptors and illustrators). New York: Alfred A. Knopf, 1962.
The Ring by Richard Wagner. John Updike and Warren Chappell (adaptors and illustrators). New York: Alfred A. Knopf, 1964.
Three Texts from Early Ipswich: A Pageant. Ipswich, Massachusetts: Seventeenth Century Day Committee of the Town of Ipswich, 1968.
Bottom's Dream: Adapted from William Shakespeare's A Midsummer Night's Dream. John Updike, editor. New York: Alfred A. Knopf, 1969.

SECONDARY SOURCES

ADLER, RENATA. "Arcadia, Pa.," *The New Yorker*, XXXIX (April 13, 1963), 182-88. An analysis of *The Centaur* that shows convincingly the successful combination of myth and realistic narrative.
BRENNER, GERRY. "John Updike's Criticism of the Return to Nature," *Twentieth Century Literature*, XII (April, 1966), 3-14. An excellent study that focuses on *Rabbit, Run* and the tension between urban life and natural events.
DETWEILER, ROBERT. "John Updike and the Indictment of Culture-Protestantism." *Four Spiritual Crises in Mid-Century American Fiction*. Gainesville: University of Florida Press, 1964. A study

of *Rabbit, Run* from the perspective of Reinhold Niebuhr's theology.

—————. "Updike's *Couples*: Eros Demythologized," *Twentieth Century Literature*, XVII (October, 1971), 235-46. Relates *Couples* to de Rougemont's *Love in the Western World* and *Love Declared*.

DOYLE, PAUL. "Updike's Fiction: Motifs and Techniques," *Catholic World*, LXLIX (September, 1964), 356-62. Argues in favor of Updike's artistic skill as a means of presenting a significant moral message.

FINKELSTEIN, SIDNEY. *Existentialism and Alienation in American Literature*. New York: International Publishers, 1965. Brief discussion of *Rabbit, Run* and *The Centaur* that portrays Updike as an alienated Existentialist and sees Harry Angstrom and George Caldwell as extensions of that alienated spirit.

GALLOWAY, DAVID. *The Absurd Hero in American Fiction*. Austin: University of Texas Press, 1966. Sound discussion of *The Poorhouse Fair*, *Rabbit, Run*, and *The Centaur* in a chapter on Updike entitled "The Absurd Man as Saint."

HAMILTON, ALICE and HAMILTON, KENNETH. *The Elements of John Updike*. Grand Rapids: Wm. B. Eerdmans Publishing Company, 1970. The only book-length study of Updike, marred by religious symbol hunting and overattention to tenuous religious allusions in Updike's fiction and poetry.

HARPER, HOWARD M. JR. *Desperate Faith: A Study of Bellow, Salinger, Mailer, Baldwin, and Updike*. Chapel Hill: The University of North Carolina Press, 1967. Fairly successful study of the spiritual effect of Updike's fiction in a secular world.

MIZENER, ARTHUR. *The Sense of Life in the Modern Novel*. Boston: Houghton Mifflin, 1964. Sensitive and sensible analysis of Peter Caldwell in a chapter called "The American Hero as High School Boy." Argues that Updike's style and subject matter clash and that this dissonance is typical of American life.

O'CONNOR, WILLIAM VAN. "John Updike and William Styron." Harry T. Moore, ed. *Contemporary American Novelists*. Carbondale: Southern Illinois University Press, 1964. Assesses Updike as a novelist with greater potential than Styron.

PODHORETZ, NORMAN. *Doings and Undoings*. New York: Farrar, Straus, 1964. A hostile evaluation of Updike in a chapter called "A Dissent on Updike." Says that Updike is immature, lacking in imagination, and unable to create credible characters.

SAMUELS, CHARLES THOMAS. "The Art of Fiction, XLIII: John Updike," *The Paris Review*, XII (Winter, 1968), 84-117. A fascinating interview in which Updike comments on his career as author, on *Couples, Rabbit, Run,* and on other American writers.

TANNER, TONY. *City of Words: American Fiction 1950-1970.* New York: Harper & Row, Publishers, 1971. Intelligent commentary on *The Poorhouse Fair, Rabbit, Run, The Centaur,* and *Couples* in a chapter entitled "A Compromised Environment."

"View from the Catacombs," *Time,* XCI (April 26, 1968), 66-75. Cover story on Updike following the publication of *Couples* and viewing Updike as a force in changing American morals.

WARD, JOHN A. "John Updike's Fiction," *Critique,* V (Spring-Summer, 1962), 27-41. Generally favorable appraisal of Updike as novelist; negative assessment of *Rabbit, Run* and of *New Yorker* influence on Updike.

The annotated bibliography of secondary source works above is representative, not comprehensive. Other works that I have consulted are listed in "Notes and References."

Index

179